Tending
PEOPLE

Tending PEOPLE

PORTRAIT OF A CAREER IN HR

MARSHA YOUNG

XULON PRESS ELITE

Xulon Press
2301 Lucien Way #415
Maitland, FL 32751
407.339.4217
www.xulonpress.com

© 2021 by Marsha Young

All rights reserved solely by the author. The author guarantees all contents are original and do not infringe upon the legal rights of any other person or work. No part of this book may be reproduced in any form without the permission of the author. The views expressed in this book are not necessarily those of the publisher.

Due to the changing nature of the Internet, if there are any web addresses, links, or URLs included in this manuscript, these may have been altered and may no longer be accessible. The views and opinions shared in this book belong solely to the author and do not necessarily reflect those of the publisher. The publisher therefore disclaims responsibility for the views or opinions expressed within the work.

Unless otherwise indicated, Scripture quotations taken from the Holy Bible, New International Version (NIV). Copyright © 1973, 1978, 1984, 2011 by Biblica, Inc.™. Used by permission. All rights reserved.

Scripture quotations taken from the New King James Version (NKJV). Copyright © 1982 by Thomas Nelson, Inc. Used by permission. All rights reserved.

Paperback ISBN-13: 978-1-6628-2437-1
Ebook ISBN-13: 978-1-6628-2438-8

Table of Contents

Preface	Tending People	vii
Chapter One	Leadership without Lipstick	1
Chapter Two	Herding Cats	13
Chapter Three	Choking on the Tension	18
Chapter Four	Standing Room Only	29
Chapter Five	Welcome – Glad You Are Here	35
Chapter Six	Holes in Stockings and Stories	41
Chapter Seven	No Good Deed Goes Unpunished	50
Chapter Eight	Grease Pits and Power Plays	62
Chapter Nine	Journey into the Grease Pit	69
Chapter Ten	Dress For Success – Or Not	82
Chapter Eleven	Caring Not Coddling	93
Chapter Twelve	A Rotten Attitude Stinks	106
Chapter Thirteen	Dazed and Confused	114
Chapter Fourteen	Power in Ruby Red Slippers	124
Chapter Fifteen	Importance vs. Value	136
Chapter Sixteen	Let the Good Times Roll	145
Chapter Seventeen	More Good Times … or Something	156
Chapter Eighteen	Weep With Those Who Weep	162
Chapter Nineteen	The Secret Stash	171
Chapter Twenty	Clever But Clueless	179
Conclusion	Pulling Into the Station	187
Notes		197
Bibliography		199
About the author		201

I wanted to write this book because it is my growing conviction that my life belongs to others just as much as it belongs to myself and that what is experienced as most unique often proves to be most solidly embedded in the common condition of being human.

Henri Nouwen, *Reaching Out*[1]

Tend – 1) to take care of; minister to; watch over; look after; attend to 2) to be in charge of or at work at; manage or operate. *Webster's New World Dictionary: Third College Edition.*[2]

Preface
TENDING PEOPLE

Work. Not just labor as an abstract subject, but the actual performance, the experience, the fascination of it. The look, feel and smell of it. The nature of work itself has interested me all of my life. How do we make our way in the world? How do we acquire a skill, develop an expertise which will allow us to achieve the life we want?

I have observed glass-blowers at work in Ireland and watched oil drillers from atop a drilling platform on the wind swept plains of Texas. As a human resources executive, I have seen the Golden Gate Bridge through the window of my own office on the 32nd floor of a skyscraper in downtown San Francisco. And as a young temporary worker, I remember the smell and cool surface of the stalks and leaves as I cleaned and packed strawberry plants in a packing shed. I came from "working class" people. Everyone I knew worked. It was a point of pride if they did it well. It was a source of embarrassment if they were incompetent or slackers.

We are told that man's first workplace was a garden. His assignment was to tend it. To tend anything requires attention, effort and a certain kindness; that is, a sensitivity to the impact of one's actions and attitudes upon that which is being tended. This can be as applicable in tending people as in tending plants.

I once read of a monk who, during the middle ages, taught that in order to produce a well-tended garden, one must first realize that what is needed is not a scepter but a hoe. Unfortunately, in many work places we have an abundance of those who think they are wielding a scepter, ruling and reigning mostly in their own imaginations; when what is desperately needed are those who are willing and able to take up a hoe. Tending people is a learning process and we never learn it all. It is a skills based endeavor and only the most skillful ever really accomplish much. It is a test of personal integrity and not everyone earns a passing grade.

These pages are an attempt to describe tending people in a way that may be helpful, especially if you also happen to earn your livelihood coaching colleagues, mentoring those on a work team, leading a department, or even an entire workforce. Perhaps you will discover an approach you have not yet tried. If you tend to be a corrective coach, perhaps you will learn the benefits of a more collaborative approach. If, however, your natural bent is to be a collaborative counselor, maybe you will find some increased effectiveness in knowing when and how to take a more corrective stance. Maybe you will discover that listening, not just for information but also for mutual understanding or for forming a stronger connection with another, is a valuable use of your time. As a person of faith, it is also my attempt to communicate how one can bring one's faith to bear upon our professional responsibilities in a way that is respectful and rewarding.

We who are people-tenders, that is those of us who labor in the helping professions, or as team leaders and supervisors, managers and mentors, sometimes forget that those being tended are first and foremost people. They are not fungible widgets nor game pieces to be moved about on the board at the mover's whim. Often they are people who have agreed to give us their time and talent in exchange for something of value to them, frequently wages. But this does not automatically mean that they will give us their best, nor that we who to tend them will necessarily deserve the best they have to offer.

That kind of reciprocal working relationship requires careful tending. It is a valuable commodity and can rise to become a sacred trust. Max DePree in his seminal work, *Leadership Is An Art*, calls it a "covenantal relationship":

> *A covenantal relationship rests on shared commitment to ideas, to issues, to values, to goals ... Covenantal relationships tolerate risk and forgive errors."* [3]

Someone once said to me, if you have one employee you have one problem and if you have one thousand employees you have one thousand problems. I disagree. Yes, tending people can, and not infrequently does, include the possibility of real frustration with undesirable behaviors; but there is also the potential for genuine collaboration, for the mutual satisfaction of a job well done.

I considered it a privilege to be charged with coaching, counseling and leading people. Much has been written on leadership, but perhaps too much attention has been paid to it. I wonder whether we might not be better off paying more heed to enhancing and rewarding good follower-ship if you will. Be that as it may, I found that my primary interest lay in neither leadership nor follower-ship; but rather in the challenges and occasional chaos of tending people. I discovered courage among those I would not have expected to exhibit it. Sadly, I sometimes found fear tactics and power games being played right where I suspected them to exist. Of course, along the way there was some good humor and occasionally an incident so completely bizarre that it could only fall under the category of "you simply cannot make this stuff up."

The following chapters contain stories drawn from my years in human resource (HR) management. The stories are not necessarily in chronological order, but roughly follow my career path from early years to the end. Although all names have been changed, and where necessary personal identifying details have been obscured, the events occurred as described, even those that strain credulity. You will also find at the end of each chapter one or two Tending Tips, ideas and thoughts you may find useful.

It is my hope that readers may find some encouragement as they read this account of tending people. For me it was a worthwhile journey. I hope that it may be for you as well.

Chapter One

LEADERSHIP WITHOUT LIPSTICK

On a bright, sunny, Monday morning, the conference room was packed and the atmosphere was tense. A new vice president of operations, Susan, had just joined the region and this was to be her first staff meeting with the team leaders whom she had inherited. As the regional HR manager, I had already met Susan – and trust me, no one called her Sue – and I knew that we were all in for a bumpy ride. My boss, Janet, the regional Sr. VP, who was also Susan's boss, had asked me to sit in and observe the meeting.

Susan introduced herself briefly, quickly touching upon her own fairly impressive background, including a couple of advanced degrees and several years running a Bay Area hospital complex, which was well respected in the industry. She made it clear that she considered personal data superfluous to the business at hand, and then rapidly launched into her heightened expectations of those present. She did not ask anyone else to introduce themselves, nor did she ask a single question about their backgrounds, specific skills, or special areas of expertise. She had read their files and knew all she needed to know. Or so she thought. The meeting was a disaster as Susan's new subordinates filed out, after forty-five grueling minutes of being lectured, with every tooth in each of their heads on edge.

Susan's boss, Janet, called me later that afternoon to ask how I thought the introductory staff meeting had gone. I tried to make politically correct hemming and hawing noises, at which I was never very good. I lamely offered, "It's going to take some time, but Susan seems determined to make a difference." Janet was having none of it.

"I asked for your honest opinion about how Susan's first staff meeting went. That is what I expect you to give me. She is new to the region and I have given her a big assignment with a lot riding on her ability to elicit some critical contributions from her team. So, again, how did it go?"

Sometimes I hated my job. Yes, I knew about managing upward and telling truth to power and other such similar drivel. Just once, couldn't I have said something soothing and moved on? Apparently not.

So I tried to ease into telling Janet the truth. "Well, the good news is that she was on time, well-organized, and clearly knew her stuff."

"Okay, so what was the problem?" Janet asked.

"Most of them left the room already disliking her and inclined to dragging their feet."

My boss voiced her dismay and skepticism. She knew Susan from a prior company, knew for a fact that she was smart, hardworking, and able to "get the job done."

I explained that none of that was at issue. What was at issue was whether Susan was going to be able to get these people to follow her lead. At the moment it was not looking promising. I further explained that she had begun by ignoring everyone in the room and making herself the center of attention. She did not ask questions, she gave orders; she interrupted others when they tried to offer a suggestion, and demeaned their understanding of our customer base by stating that she had come from an operation twice the size of ours, and knew how things were done in the big leagues. I concluded by saying that, if I had read the room accurately, her staff was already hoping she would find our little pond too small for her big duck's ego and go back to wherever she came from. Other than that, it had gone just swimmingly. There was an ominous silence from the other end of the line.

I was not privy to whatever discussions took place over the next two weeks between Susan and Janet. They were both based primarily out of the San Francisco office (even though most of Susan's team was located in the Sacramento office where her staff meetings were held). I also worked primarily out of the Sacramento office, although I had an office in the San Francisco location as well. All I knew was that, after a brief call from Janet, I was instructed to meet with Susan and begin to coach her, after each staff meeting, to see if I could help her become more effective in connecting with her team. It seemed that Janet had received feedback similar to my own from several other people, and Susan was now being viewed as a questionable hire. She was earning six figures, with a five figure bonus option, and she simply did not know how to form an effective working relationship with her team.

Two weeks later, on a drizzly Monday morning, Susan's staff filed glumly into the same conference room, looking for all the world like recalcitrant teenagers being sent to the principal's office. It might have been funny, if it were not so critical. Susan was a senior level hire, brought into a division that had lost market share for the prior three quarters; and it was expected that she would be able to turn things around in less than a year. So far the only turn-around being anticipated was her own, out the same door she had entered, along with their fervent hopes that it *would* hit her on the way out.

I had not been involved in her recruitment, but rather she had been "sprung on me" as a surprise senior executive hire. It did not happen often, but when it did, I sometimes found myself caught between a rock I did not know, and a hard place I had not chosen.

We took our places, agendas at the ready, and waded into the first item. I had taken a seat at the far end of the table, in order to have a full view of all the participants, as well as to be able to make eye contact with Susan, who was seated at the head of the table. I was to serve as her counterpoint, check and balance, or pain in her backside, depending upon your point of view. I did not consider this to be a plum assignment, but it was work that needed to be done, and it had been determined that I was the one to do it.

Susan began to hold forth and as I glanced up toward the far end of the table to make eye contact with her to attempt to get her to tone down the rhetoric ("*If* you have read the latest reports, *surely* you realize what we need, etc.,") when I noticed to my chagrin that her front teeth were smeared with lipstick. Bright red.

I wasn't the only one who noticed, and various glances and a couple of titters made their way around the table. It has been my experience that a lot of adolescent behavior goes on at corporate conference tables, poorly disguised as humor. Nevertheless, Susan, oblivious to more than just her stained front teeth, continued her remarks.

"What we need are new stretch goals," she announced with authority. "I am not talking about a little edge-out goal here, but a real down and dirty, put your neck on the line, kind of stretch goal. Now how are we going to identify: a) what those are and, b) how we are going to achieve them?"

There was a thick silence. No one spoke and few looked up from their notes.

"Come on, people. I know at least one or two of you must have some ideas. Let's hear them."

More paper shuffling and foot scuffling, but no one offered a "stretch" goal. So Susan determinedly got up and went to the white board, where she began to rapidly dash off about five or six potential goals for the team. Actually a few of them were not half bad, not that anyone sitting there was prepared to admit it.

Finally, one of the bolder members made a half-hearted comment, followed by a couple of others who joined in with tepid assent. The meeting stumbled on like this for another half an hour, at which point Susan dismissed the lot of them with a disgusted, "Okay, give it some thought and get back to me. I have to say, though, that I am disappointed in what I have heard this morning. This isn't going to get us to where we need to be."

I could only hope that she did not hear the muttered "Couldn't have said it better myself," from one of the more experienced supervisors as he trudged out of the room. I had taken more than a few notes myself during this little stop, drop, and roll exercise, and I was not looking forward to reviewing them with the redoubtable Susan. But it was a job and I had drawn the short straw on this day.

After a quick rest stop and coffee refill, Susan and I met in my office to review the meeting. Such is corporate life, a meeting to review a meeting. I almost wished I had a headache and could go home. But the reality was that I almost never had actual headaches, and the ones I did have generally showed up wearing expensive suits and carrying a briefcase absolutely empty of any vestige of self-awareness. In Susan's case, her six hundred dollar Jimmy Choo's only added insult to injury. Of course, they could have been knock-offs and I would not have known the difference.

But while I could not tell fake designer footwear from genuine, I could usually tell the difference between posturing and real leadership. It was something like running internal facial-recognition software. You might not know exactly what you were looking for, but when all the points lined up, you recognized it when you saw it.

Being the go-getter that she was, Susan did not wait for me to say anything, but rather jumped right in with, "So I understand my first meeting two weeks ago could have gone better and that you have been asked to give me some pointers on improving my connection with my team. So, lay it on me. How was today's meeting? I think it showed some improvement from the first one, don't you?" Clearly she was a football fan and believed that the best defense was a good offense.

Here is where my paradigm was different from many practicing my profession. I did not believe that power and money alone were all that were necessary to produce good results in business. Yes, leaders needed to possess some authority to make and implement decisions; but when coupled with appreciation and respect for others, even better results were often produced. I had prayed about this encounter the night before, and I sent up another one in my thoughts. *Help me to be of some genuine value to her, and to do her no harm even if I do have to hurt her feelings. Let me speak the truth to her, but without cruelty or arrogance.*

"Susan, I appreciate your energetic approach and your willingness to listen to feedback. I have read your file, one of the perks and hazards of being in HR, so I am somewhat familiar with what you bring to the table. Before we go over this morning's staff meeting, I have a few things I would like to ask you."

"Sure, fire away."

I asked her what she thought her best job skill was and after about a split second she replied, "I know how to analyze the data and act upon it."

Note to self: She values data and action. People not so much. I acknowledged that that was a valuable tool and then surprised her by asking, "Why do you think you were hired?"

She said it was to bring the numbers back up and increase market share.

"And just how does that get done?" I asked.

She looked momentarily annoyed, her expression clearly indicating "I always knew these HR people were dead weight," and replied, "First we determine where the low-hanging fruit is, and go after that. Then we look at where we have lost business, and go back and try to regain it. Finally, we will examine where we can best target business expansion."

"Do you realize that you just used the word 'we' several times in that sentence? I take it that you do not intend to accomplish all this alone. Correct?"

Now she looked more than mildly irritated. "Of course not," she snapped at me.

"Well, just now that is a problem for you, because not a single member of your team is currently willing to help you accomplish what you just described to me."

She sat there looking somewhat taken aback and sputtered with a good deal of asperity, "Why in the world not? Don't they realize their bonuses, or even their jobs, depend upon it?"

"Yes, they are aware of that. Nevertheless, they won't help you, because they don't like you. Oh, they will give you the bare minimum; but beyond that, not much." I stated this as a fact, not a threat, as respectfully as I could.

"What?" she exploded. "They don't even know me. I've only been here a month."

I then asked her which of her newly acquired team members she liked best. She said she really could not say, because she did not know them that well ... yet.

"So you are annoyed that they do not like you, given that they do not know you, and yet you are clear that you really couldn't say whether you like any of them, precisely because you do not know them well enough. Am I hearing you correctly?"

Understanding began to dawn. Bosses often forget that between themselves and their subordinates it is never a level playing field. Forget all the speeches about open door policies and safe places to vent. When the rubber meets the road, one person has power over the other and neither of them is likely to forget it. One of them is always going to feel more vulnerable than the other and trust will be in short supply until it has been earned. Furthermore, humility builds bridges while arrogance burns them.

Susan was finally ready to listen and the real conversation began. I asked whether she realized that she had insulted them, more than once, during the meeting that morning, and had demeaned them, however unintentionally. Still relatively clueless she asked, "When, how?"

"One example would be when you told the group that surely *at least* one or two of them might have a few ideas. That indicated that you believed most of them were devoid of any ideas at all, and that the one or two who might have something to offer, were likely to offer inadequate ideas. How likely would you be to jump into that kind of invitation with your own superior?"

"I wouldn't," Susan responded without hesitation.

"Exactly. And you have more experience and education than many of your team members. Nevertheless, you would feel hesitant to offer a suggestion, if your boss put it to you in the terms you used."

"Okay, point taken. What else?" Susan was nothing if not sturdy.

"While I believe you intended to come across as issuing a challenge, instead it sounded more like you were throwing down a gauntlet. It was not just your words, it was your tone and your cadence."

"Oh, please," she responded as she barely suppressed an eye roll. "Tone and cadence? What are we running here, a debate club or a business?"

Barely suppressing my own eye-roll and sigh, I responded, "We are running a business that depends upon the people you met with this morning to do their jobs, and not just by sleepwalking through their routines, but by giving you the very best they've got. When your tone is arrogant, and I'm sorry but it was, and your speech cadence is as brisk as it was, you give them the impression that you have much more important things to do than to spend time meeting with them or listening to them."

I then shared with her an occasion years earlier, wherein I was sent from the West Coast to a Southern state to meet with a mission-critical project team which was working on something that would likely determine the future of that company for the next five years. Before leaving, I asked some trusted colleagues for suggestions on how best to influence the outcome of the upcoming discussions. I was told bluntly that I needed to slow down. My colleagues, who had worked with the southern team recently, explained that if I went into the meeting talking fast and furiously, as was my inclination, the others would view me as a know-it-all and shut down on me. They would not hear a thing I had to offer.

They also told me to be sure and offer to stay late on Friday if need be. When I asked why that particular pointer, they explained that sometimes other regions of the country thought that West Coast people were a little "too laid back" and that we often quit work at noon on Fridays, in order to get an early jump on the weekend. They also believed that most of us went surfing on the weekends. Granted they added this slightly tongue-in-cheek.

I was amazed and amused. Our offices were at least eighty miles inland from the nearest beach, and I rarely left before six p.m., even on a Friday. But I soon learned they were right on target as far as the perceptions of the Southern region regarding West Coast colleagues.

"Similarly, Susan, you are originally from the East Coast, and we are a West Coast team. Your prior corporate subculture was a little different than ours and you need to take the time to recognize and adjust for those differences. I have heard that you tend to take an in-your-face approach to problem solving. Several of your team members have been with this organization for more than a decade and they don't appreciate your approach. They need you to first acknowledge their past contributions, before you begin to challenge their current effectiveness. Your success in this region may very well depend upon whether you are willing to make this effort."

We talked further and explored how these nuances affected her lack of connection with her team. As we talked, she began to realize that I really was there to coach and to support her, not to criticize and distract her from important issues. Finally, at the end of the meeting, I mentioned the lipstick on her teeth.

She was again irritated and surprised that no one bothered to mention it to her. I told her that frankly, since the team was feeling disrespected and threatened, they chose to snicker about it behind her back, rather than politely mention it to her or ignore it. It was their secret little "gotcha" – and yes, it was juvenile. But when there is no trust or respect in a relationship, this is what happens.

We met twice a month for the next six months. She kept her job, her team began to step up their performance, and the regional market share began to creep upward. Certainly her performance was only one contributing factor to that outcome, but hers was a key factor.

A couple of years later, Susan was being transferred to another region in her role as a turn-around specialist. Shortly before she left she asked to meet with me and, although our one-on-ones had long since ended, we had maintained a casual but friendly relationship.

To my surprise, she wanted to say thank you. She told me, with a lot more humility than was in evidence two years earlier, that this assignment had been both the most difficult of her career and yet, also the most rewarding. She said she was looking forward to her new territory, and then with a smile she added, "And I have already called two or three key people in that region and asked them to help me understand the lay of the land."

Tending people takes time. It also takes goodwill. Yes, pressure must sometimes be applied, but it can be done with the healing power of understanding rather than the corrosive pressure of leverage and pecking order. There must also be willingness to tell another the uncomfortable truth. However, fairly often, telling the uncomfortable truth can become a catalyst for a more open and honest working environment. Everyone benefits when this happens. Sometimes I loved my job.

Tending Tip: We often want the satisfaction of a quick-fix, and for minor issues that may work. But complex relational issues will require taking the long view, sometimes inching along with painstaking restraint until trust is established.

Chapter Two

HERDING CATS

"You are scaring people. You have got to lighten up."

This directive was delivered to me with no small dose of irony from my boss, Glenda, because it was supposedly my ability to "scare people straight," in a professional way of course, that was a legitimate part of my duties at this Fortune 500 company. If someone needed a "good talking to" or a serious reality check about their performance, I was often the person dispatched to deliver the message.

I was serving as the regional human resources manager of a national managed care organization and I worked primarily out of the Sacramento offices. However, my duties included oversight of the San Francisco and Los Angeles offices as well, in matters pertaining to administration and HR. Layoffs were looming and I was privy to this knowledge, although I did not want to be. Without realizing it, I was race-walking up and down the lengthy aisles of the cube farm with a demeanor that did not bode well – for anyone.

In the pressure-cooker environment that precedes any significant corporate layoff, I was diligently tending to severance package analysis, job-search strategies, and customer/client implications. The WARN (Worker Adjustment Retraining and Notification Act of 1988) announcement was being developed as I sped from one strategy session to the next. WARN is a legal notification required by the federal government anytime a single employer plans to lay off fifty or more workers within a seventy-five mile radius. We were getting ready to down-size approximately three hundred jobs. It was the workplace equivalent of going nuclear.

So although I was tending to all these necessary preparations, I was not tending to our people, which was also my responsibility. And people noticed. On the day in which I was admonished to "lighten up" I took an early lunch, went to a nearby park to decompress, and gave myself a good talking-to.

Tending people is hard work. It is demands focus, energy, and the bringing to bear of every good intention you can develop. It does not happen naturally nor accidentally. If and when it happens at all, it comes about only because someone decided it needed to be done, was worth doing right, and was committed to seeing it through. I was determined to be one of those individuals. I respected the work these people had done, the way they had served our customers and clients, and the contributions they had made to the whole organization. They deserved the very best we could provide to them during the difficult weeks ahead. It was a debt of integrity which management owed to loyal employees.

That same afternoon, I slowed down my pace – of walking, of breathing, and even of thinking about all that had to be accomplished in the coming weeks and months. As they say in baseball, when the pitcher is jittery with a full count and there are two runners on in a tie game, it was time to slow the game down.

It made a difference, as I engaged more with others instead of carrying on a frantic internal dialogue about whether I had remembered to file a certain form or notify a particular government agency.

Employees began to smile a little more and snipe at each other a little less as the tension level dropped a bit lower. And they began to openly ask more questions about what was happening and how it might affect them personally; because despite all the well-meaning efforts to keep "the big secret" as Benjamin Franklin said, "Three may keep a secret, if two of them are dead."[4]

When employees are whispering to each other about – well, they are not sure what about, but they are pretty sure it is not good – then things quickly deteriorate into rumor and fear-mongering. During times of organizational distress there simply cannot be too much communication. And communication should not just come from the top down. Peer groups, departmental get-togethers, and one-on-ones, were all critical as we prepared to disrupt the work lives of three hundred people.

In John 10:12-13, were are told that the hired man runs away from the wolf because he is only working for pay. He does not care for the sheep; but the shepherd genuinely cares. Tending people in the workplace can look a lot like shepherding. Yes, it also sometimes looks like herding cats. Feels like it, too, when fur is flying all over the place and hisses and raised backs are on full display. However, when goodwill is brought to bear upon the situation people will often respond well.

Over the next few months we conducted mock job interviews for those who would soon be going on real ones. We offered workshops to help employees brush up on their technical skills. And we allowed them to use paid company time to go on job interviews weeks before they were actually to be laid off. And it all paid off. We kept track of who landed where and under what circumstances. Ultimately we were able to help over 90% of our displaced employees gain new employment. And 75% of them obtained jobs that paid at or above what they had been earning with us. I was told these percentages were well above industry averages. Now that felt like some productive people tending.

On a personal footnote, my own job was eliminated during this down-sizing as headquarters decided to close down the entire region. It was all part of a national re-centralization effort. I sometimes pictured this particular dynamic as resembling a big corporate rubber band. Every few years headquarters would decide that decentralization was the way to go. Let's open some regional offices, give people in the field a little more autonomy. So the rubber band would be stretched out a little. And that would work well for a few years. But inevitably, either someone would go off the rails, or some major financial crisis would occur, and headquarters would decide it was time to pull in the reins and re-centralize the operation. Let's regather decision-making power back here at headquarters. Those people out there in the field couldn't find a strategic goal with a GPS locator. The rubber band would contract again.

Corporate headquarters, located in the Midwest, had generously offered me the possibility of a transfer and likely promotion. But my family was located in the area where I worked and I did not feel like uprooting my whole life, so I thanked them for the offer but declined.

One of my final tasks was literally to turn in my keys and "lay myself off." It was an experience that would be of considerable value to me in the coming years, particularly when I counseled someone who was facing job loss.

Tending Tips:
- Job loss is a very big deal to most people, but it is not the end of the world. How their employment ends greatly impacts how they will move forward. You can be a confidence-building influence during that process.
- If it is your job that is ending, take stock of everything you have learned during the process. Think about how you felt, what you worried about or simply wondered about, what actions by others were most helpful to you as you processed job loss. Use that knowledge to assist others as you go forward.

Chapter Three
CHOKING ON THE TENSION

It is never a good thing when your phone rings and the manager on the other end says, "We have a serious problem."

However, the nature of my role in the company meant that I was destined to receive more calls about problems, specifically people problems, than just about anyone else in that organization. This was particularly true during the years when I specialized in employee relations.

I asked the first question that should always be asked, "Is anyone hurt?"

On any given day we had several hundred employees in the field doing difficult and sometimes dangerous work. Work that could get them killed if they did not apply their safety training and pay attention to what they were doing.

The reluctant reply I received was that everyone was now safe, but an employee had almost been seriously injured and another employee was at fault. My caller, Sidney (usually called Sid) was the manager of both employees and I knew him to be a competent and confident individual, with years of experience in managing outside plant personnel; so I was surprised to hear a note of near panic in his voice.

"Well, accidents will happen in your line of work." I replied. "Tell me what happened, Sid, and what I can do to help."

There was a moment of dead silence, and then he blurted out, "That is the worst part of it. It was no accident. There was a disagreement in the field as one of my crew was getting ready to climb." (Their work required climbing very high structures.) "Two guys got into it, Dane and Crandall, and ... well ... there was a scuffle, Dane lost his temper and ... well ... he choked Crandall."

"Excuse me? Do you mean he actually put his hands on a coworker and choked his neck?"

I knew what the words "choked him" meant but this was the first time I had ever heard those words applied to an interaction between two of our own employees, and I was having some difficulty processing what I was hearing. Ours was a pretty civil work place; where people said "please" and "thank you" as a matter of course. So to hear that one of them had attacked another was completely unexpected. Of course, this was a time when workplace violence was still a rare occurrence, not the routine thing requiring full lock-down drills that it later became.

Sid began to recount who, what, where, when details. He finished up with an anguished question. "Do I have to fire him? Dane is usually a good employee, and he is really a skillful technician. I just cannot afford to lose him, especially with the work load we are carrying right now."

After determining that he had sent Dane home until further notice, and that he had made sure Crandall, the fellow who had been choked, had been sent to a doctor to be checked out; we discussed what to do next.

We talked about potential liability, if Crandall decided he wanted to sue the company. We discussed whether Crandall had some responsibility for the altercation (he had) and whether any disciplinary action was going to be necessary for him. Finally, we circled back around to the thorny heart of the matter: what to do with Dane?

The easy answer was to fire him. He had instigated the argument, according to two other crew members who were present. Yes, Crandall got in his face, but only after Dane had been "ragging on him" for half the shift. Dane also took the first swing, and while Crandall did not walk away as he could have, and he had landed one good punch, Dane was clearly the one who was mostly to blame for the incident. All this said nothing of the fact that he had choked a coworker. This simply could not be tolerated.

However, Dane had ten years with the company, was known to be a hard worker with good skills, and he had no prior disciplinary actions other than one written warning from two years prior. It was also related to his temper though, and now this? We were on solid ground for termination. It would protect the company from much of the potential liability associated with this kind of behavior, if management came down "hard and fast" on Dane.

This may seem harsh to readers who have never been on the administrative end of corporate liability; but the fact is that if we retained Dane, and he ever did anything like this again, well ... as our legal counsel might have said, it would be time to "get out the checkbook and start writing zeroes behind the first number." The employment law theory behind such liability is known as "negligent retention." This meant you had kept someone employed, when you knew they might be a threat, particularly if later they did, in fact, harm or endanger another. Still, Sid, his manager was reluctant to fire him. Was there anything I could do?

I was not sure there was an alternative, but I said I would give it some thought and get back to him. About an hour later I called him and asked him to call Dane at home and tell him to be in my office at nine o'clock the next morning. I could have met with Dane at the close of that same day, but I wanted him to sit at home and think about what he had done and about what it could cost him, before I approached him with his options. Sometimes we are too quick to try to fix the problem, when what we need to do is let the problem "sit" for a while. This is not avoidance, it is patience.

Anger management. It is a cliché in our society. It is a Robert DeNiro movie, for crying out loud. Guys who did the kind of hard physical work that Dane did had very little use for touchy-feely stuff like "anger management." It was going to be a tough conversation.

Dane walked into my office right on the dot of nine o'clock the next morning. His company uniform shirt was well-pressed, his hair was neatly combed, and his face showed some faint bruising on one cheek. He was a large man in his early thirties with strong looking arms and big hands. They were not a pair of hands you would want to see around anyone's throat. He was not happy to be there, understandably, but he wasn't defiant either; as I had more-or-less expected him to be. In fact, he looked tired and defeated.

After exchanging greetings, we got down to it. I let him know that, per company policy, he was entitled to have his manager, or a trusted coworker present, but he declined. I asked him if he knew how serious his situation was and he said he thought he did.

"Dane, can you tell me what you think is about to happen here?"

"I suppose you are going to fire me," he replied in a dull voice.

"Well, that would certainly be understandable, and it could still happen. You violated company policy, and you put another employee at risk. But let me ask you this, Dane. If we can find a way through this, and allow you to maintain your employment, would you be willing to do some very hard work to make that happen? Are you willing to take full responsibility for your actions?"

He looked at me with an odd combination of suspicion and a flicker of hope. One of the few things I had working for me in this situation was that in the years I had been with the company I had gained a reputation for being fair. Not a push-over, not a bleeding heart, but fair. This had been precipitated by the very first employee disciplinary action to which I was assigned some years before the current Dane crisis.

I had been with the company for less than a month, when my manager assigned me to conduct a termination meeting with a front line employee and his supervisor. The supervisor, Rocky, had asked that I meet with him in his office to conduct the meeting, to spare Gene, the employee being fired, the company equivalent of a "perp walk" – leaving the human resources offices after being let go.

My manager, Helen, had already informed Rocky that Gene was going to be terminated following a serious customer complaint regarding a theft; however, due to a scheduling conflict she could not conduct the meeting. I was being sent to complete the process and fill out the necessary paperwork. When I got back to our offices about an hour and a half later, Helen asked whether the termination had gone smoothly.

"Not exactly."

"What do you mean," she asked. "I hope Gene didn't give you any real trouble."

"No," I replied. "He didn't. But then I didn't fire him either."

"But that was the whole purpose of the meeting. Wasn't I clear about that?"

"Oh, you were clear. But I asked him a few questions about the allegation against him. It was obvious that Rocky thought Gene was getting a raw deal and did not believe his guy should be fired. So I asked Gene to tell me exactly what had happened. He did and then I asked him some very pointed questions, each of which he answered fully and with a lot of detail."

People who are lying to you usually stick to a vague story and "can't remember" much detail, but they will talk a lot – without really saying anything. By contrast, those telling the truth will usually remember very specific details, what time of day it was, background noises like a TV program, what someone was wearing, that kind of thing. And they will often only reply to the question being asked, but will not offer elaborate spin theories.

"By the end of the meeting," I told her, "I was convinced Gene was telling the truth and that he did not take the diamond ring he was accused of stealing. I had read his file; his record was clean and his evaluations were consistently good. So I told him that I was not ending his employment, and that I would look into this further and get back to him and Rocky with a final decision within two days. I hope you are okay with that."

After her initial surprise, Helen just said, "Well, I hired you to think, not just take orders. Good for you."

After further investigation into the customer complaint, it was established that Gene did not take a valuable diamond ring, as the customer had alleged. In fact, it turned out that this particular customer had a little insurance scam going, whereby she would have a customer repair person come into her home, and then quickly thereafter "discover" something missing. We filed a police report, and they contacted her insurance company. It turned out this wasn't the first such "theft" she had reported over the years regarding service personnel from other local companies. It was just the first time she got caught.

Gene kept his job and I suddenly gained some "street cred" for having taken the time to listen to the employee, and consider that he might be innocent and that the customer might actually be wrong. While I believed in rules, I did not believe in blindly following orders without trying to listen to everyone involved and then taking another look from a different angle. HR represented the company in disciplinary matters, but that did not mean that we automatically assumed the employee was in the wrong. We would, and often did, advocate for them when appropriate. While I did not say anything to anyone, other than to Helen, about this incident, Rocky and Gene evidently had and word quickly got around. Thus, Dane entered my office with some respect, if not optimism, for the process.

He first asked whether I realized that the incident was not solely his fault. I explained that we realized Crandall bore some responsibility in the matter, but that that was a separate issue and would be handled by Sid. We were not here to discuss anyone but him. I then asked again whether he would be willing to do some hard work in order to keep his job.

"Yeah, I need my job. I have a wife and two kids to support. You tell me what I need to do and I'll do it."

I explained how company-mandated counseling worked. Dane would see an outside counselor, who specialized in workplace issues. The counselor had no ties to the company other than being paid a fee for his services. Neither Dane's manager, nor HR (in this case, me) would ever see or hear what he discussed with his counselor. He would, however, be required to sign-in for each session, and I would be allowed to contact the counselor to confirm he was attending all required sessions.

Additionally, he would have to sign a release form in which he also acknowledged that failure to attend these sessions, or any repeat of the behavior that had caused this mess (with no ifs, ands, or buts) would result in his immediate termination without any further avenue for appeal. Was he clear about these conditions?

He naturally had a few questions. He wondered whether he would be allowed to work during the period of mandatory counseling. I told him that he would initially be suspended without pay for two weeks. During that time he would attend intensive counseling sessions, daily to begin with. After that, if the counselor agreed he was ready, he would be allowed to return to work on a strictly probationary status. He would continue to attend counseling sessions, once a week after work, for approximately three months. Co-workers would be told nothing of this arrangement and HR would keep it strictly confidential. Only his manager would know. He agreed.

Dane succeeded in completing his program, never missed a single session, and worked for the company for many more years. That was a good thing, in my estimation. But it was not the best outcome. What came later was even better.

About nine months later, I was deep in some work at my desk and did not hear anyone approach. It was after five o'clock and most people had left for the day. A light knock on my open door caused me to look up. My unexpected visitor was Dane. I had not seen him personally since the day we met to have him sign his disciplinary action agreeing to two weeks without pay. Sid, his manager, was present during that meeting and had regretfully accepted Dane's ID badge, access card to the vehicle yard, and the keys to his company truck. During his two-week suspension he would not be allowed on company property. It had been a tough, but hopeful, discussion and at least it wasn't a termination meeting.

I knew from my weekly phone calls to his counselor that he had successfully attended all his required counseling sessions and I was glad for him. However, given the proud nature of these rough and tumble outside plant guys, and the humiliating nature of our two meetings, I had not expected to see Dane again, other than perhaps at departmental meetings with fifty or more employees present. Nevertheless, there he stood, smiling hesitantly and asking if I had a minute.

"Sure, have a seat. How are you doing?" I asked.

"I'm doing ok. Much better in fact. I came by today to say thank you."

Now that caught me by surprise. In light of our previous interactions, I could not imagine that he thought very highly of my function within the organization. I imagined he saw me as, at best, a kind of necessary evil in the work place, despite the fact that I had always treated him with dignity.

"Well, that's nice, Dane, and you're welcome. But what for?"

"For saving my marriage."

I sat there touched and grateful as he told me how he had grown up with an angry father, who often took out his anger on Dane. Dane in turn became an angry adult, and despite having a pretty good marriage with two healthy kids, a well-paid job, and the respect of his co-workers, he often found himself lashing out for little or no reason at all. Just before the incident that had resulted in his mandatory counseling, he and his wife had been discussing a separation. She could not tolerate his angry outbursts any longer; as she was worried about the effect it was having on their children. With his background, Dane admitted he would have likely gone through a divorce rather than seek help. But he could not face losing his job. The mandatory anger management counseling had not only allowed him to keep his job, it had opened the door to exploring the root issues which resulted in his anger. Eventually, he and his wife began to see a counselor together and they were now determined to repair their relationship.

"So I just stopped by to say thank you. Not just for my job. But you saved my marriage too, by requiring me to go to counseling."

"I appreciate that, Dane. But obviously I didn't save your marriage. You and your wife are doing that by working through the things that could ruin it. And good for you both. I'm glad that we were able to point you in a good direction."

We parted with a warm handshake. For all the remaining years we both worked there, whenever I ran into Dane, he gave me a smile and nod. Nothing more, of course, because the guys on the crew were around and they would not understand a tough guy like him being chummy with HR. I went home that evening thankful for the opportunity to help someone make some life changes that meant two young children were going to have a chance to grow up with both parents in a healthier and happier home. Times like this I loved my job.

Tending Tips:
- When someone is giving you their version of "what happened" listen for the truth. Listen to whether they are speaking from the heart or the head. If from the heart, they may be less confident, but they will often be steadfast in their account. If speaking only from the head, they may sound clever and even convincing (in fact, they will work a little too hard to convince you) but there will be something in the account that just doesn't quite ring true. Pay attention to that.
- The physically strongest people in the work force can sometimes be the most emotionally vulnerable. When dealing with them, remember the person inside the uniform. And try to

keep in mind that they are not the job—that is just what they do for a paycheck. Who they are is a great deal more than just the job; they are husbands, wives, sons and daughters. They are worth careful consideration and they often deserve our compassion.

Chapter Four

STANDING ROOM ONLY

I t was an aging and once venerable organization that had been in business nearly one hundred years. It had originated as a family owned and operated company, but big changes had occurred in recent years, including the fact that it had gone public and was now listed on the NASDAQ stock exchange. Many employees felt the "family atmosphere" was rapidly being replaced by a more aggressive and opportunistic culture that valued profits over people. New senior management, however, saw an outdated operation badly in need of a major overhaul, if the company was to survive and thrive in the twenty-first century. Part of that overhaul was a complete review and revision of the entire compensation and benefits structure. A significant percentage of the employee base had worked for that company their entire career and they were not happy about the changes they had heard, via the rumor mill, were coming.

It was under these circumstances that I had recently joined the company. A few months into my tenure I entered a large meeting room full of hostile employees. My job was to introduce and explain the impending changes to compensation and benefits. There would be a series of such meetings until every employee had had the opportunity to hear first-hand what was coming, and to ask the questions which were on their minds. In the early years, when the company was much smaller – and when the industry competition was less threatening – the pay and pension plans had been unusually generous, beyond the industry standards of the time. Before I was asked to join this organization, I had heard the company described as a "cushy place to land," meaning the rewards were indeed generous.

The new message was a difficult one outlining significant policy changes, which in some cases meant fewer pay increases, and a moderately reduced pension plan for newer employees. The employees wanted to let the company, and me as the current spokesperson, know that they were not happy with what they had heard in advance, much of which was inaccurate. Furthermore, what they had heard in "spoiler alert" gossip was overwhelmingly negative toward the company. Some of them were feeling betrayed. Once I walked them through what the changes actually were and what they meant, and then handled Q & A for an hour about how the changes might impact them personally, the meeting ended on a more positive note. However, this was not some candy-land fantasy and before we came to that good place, one employee during the first few minutes of the meeting had called the company – and me by association–some fairly unpleasant names and had stomped out of the room.

There was an uneasy silence, where moments before there had been considerable hubbub, as they waited to see how the HR representative was going to react. The general rule in that organization was that anyone could voice an opinion in a meeting, as long as it was done with at least a modicum of respect. That did not describe what had just occurred. While I don't enjoy being insulted any more than the next person, my job was not to indulge in personal pique; I was there to present information that had considerable real-life implications for everyone present.

They wanted to know the facts about how their pay was going to be structured going forward, how much time off they could expect to accrue, and how a revised pension formula might impact their own retirement plans. After the irate guy stormed out, I waited a moment and then said, "Well, clearly he is unhappy; but he is also unwilling to listen. How about you?"

"Will you answer our questions, if we listen to you first?" someone called out.

I said that I would and added that if I did not know the answer I would tell them so. I also gave them the number for my direct line and invited them to call me with any questions that might occur to them later. By the end of that meeting, which could easily have turned into a verbal slugfest, I had gained the beginnings of respect – somewhat grudgingly – of many of those attendees. It was an instructive lesson for me in people-tending: refuse to become defensive, be honest, and offer to be available. If it is a difficult but necessary message, don't apologize and don't sugar coat it. Make every attempt to be clear without becoming combative.

Tending people requires engagement at close quarters. Whites-of-their eyes kind of stuff. It was not easy and it did not get easier as the years went on. What it did become, however, was more and more rewarding. There came a time, after a couple of years of thoughtful hard work in that company, when I could walk into an intense situation anywhere throughout that organization, and nearly everyone was willing to give me a hearing. One senior executive said to me, "You are like our organization's E.F. Hutton; when you speak, people listen." He referred to an old TV ad wherein a room full of people fell silent whenever one particular person spoke.

While I was flattered, I was not fooled. Unless the message was clear and the messenger was honest, no communication was likely have any real impact. Employees were willing to listen, not because I was stronger, smarter, or more powerful than they were; but because in between those occasionally intense situations, when things were quieter I walked the halls, stopped by lunch rooms, attended team meetings and generally made myself available to any and all. My time was their time and I listened more than I talked during those informal meetings. Then when the chips were down and the pressure was up, it gave me a space in which to stand and credibly affirm that my intentions were honest and I wanted to help. I also had a strong sense on a daily basis that I was where I was supposed to be, doing what I was meant to do. It was hard, honest work and I loved it.

I spent years working in HR keenly aware that, much like some lawyers or IRS agents, members of my profession were often considered to be either bullies or buffoons. Sometimes it was both at once, although that could be a bit of a trick to pull off. But regrettably, I have seen it done. I once knew an HR Manager who kept a small urn on her conference table, the same table where she regularly met with employees under her jurisdiction. The urn was labeled "Ashes of Terminated Employees." She thought it was funny, but I never met a single employee who agreed.

Fear, intimidation, undue leverage, all these are sometimes employed by upper-management upon those farther down the ladder. It reminded me of the old line that "He finally reached the top of the ladder, only to discover it was propped against the wrong wall." If human resources props its authority against the wall of strong-arm tactics, then we can expect nothing other than to be met with another wall of resentment. When HR goes along with such illegitimate methods, or worse still uses them, there is little possibility that the organization will be a healthy one.

However, when we use the authority the organization has vested in us to serve the greater good (that is to the benefit of the greatest number of people while avoiding harm to those who may not have as much to offer the whole) then a stronger and better focused organization is usually the result.

Weak or corrupt companies are usually known to operate on faulty principles. Ideas like:
- To get along, go along
- The Golden Rule: he who has the gold makes the rules
- Don't think – do as you're told
- Do something, even if it's wrong
- When I want your opinion, I'll give it to you.

By contrast, healthy organizations, whether they are companies, agencies, churches or clubs operate on a more open and honest set of guidelines.
- Thank you, we appreciate your feedback.
- What do you need to do your best work?
- Is there anything we can help you with?

Although I grew up in small towns, I found myself working mostly in big cities from Indianapolis to Dallas, Portland to Los Angeles. Sacramento to San Francisco was my most familiar beat and yet I still sometimes felt out of place; basically a small town square peg in a big city round hole. Nevertheless, I had opportunities to help solve problems, and to guide or mentor others in becoming a resource for their own teams. There would always be those barracudas on the job, who would gladly "eat their young" to get ahead. But there were others who wanted to learn to feed their young and mentor the less experienced among them, in order that the workplace could be more than just a job. It could foster connection, could even become a community.

So much has been written about managing people, by those with more expertise than I have, that I would hesitate to try to add anything to that dialogue. However, when it comes to tending people, there I believe I have some thoughts worth sharing.

Tending Tips:

- When confronted with a hostile person in a group, try to discern the underlying cause. Rudeness is often just fear in disguise. A bit of advice, often incorrectly attributed to Winston Churchill[5], would not go amiss in such situations, "Keep calm and carry on."[1]
- If you want career advancement, you would do well to couple it with a plan to become more skillful and generous toward those you lead or mentor. Advancement without such personal growth is just mileage.

---

[1] The slogan "Keep calm and carry on," was actually a motivational poster produced by the British government in 1939 in preparation for WWII to encourage the populace to do their duty and refuse to panic. Although over two million were produced, few were ever displayed in public. Churchill later used a paraphrase of the slogan in a speech and it became forever associated with him. The phrase gained new notoriety beginning in 2000.

Chapter Five
WELCOME! GLAD YOU ARE HERE

Early in my career, after spending a number of years as a full-time, stay-at-home mother, I was re-entering the workforce: older, not necessarily wiser, but definitely a lot more nervous. I had been hired as an office manager at a dental practice. My first day was a Tuesday (Monday had been a holiday) and when I arrived I did not see Gayle, the woman who had hired me. No one else greeted me, no one told me their name (nor did they ask for mine) until nearly an hour had elapsed. They simply trooped in and picked up charts or instruments and began their routine. Finally someone noticed me standing around and asked me, "Who are you and why are you here?"

I was nervous enough without being asked to contemplate cosmic imponderables, so I simply replied, "My name is Marsha. Gayle told me to be here at 8:30 this morning." It turned out that was all they wanted to know. Gayle was not expected until later that day, a detail she had neglected to tell me, so I spent the morning adrift, without plan or purpose, simply sitting in a corner observing the flow of traffic. Occasionally I offered to help anytime I thought there might be some small thing I could do. Perhaps I could answer a phone or file a chart.

I was also a bit chagrined to realize that everyone except me was wearing a uniform of some sort, mostly scrubs or a white lab coat. I had not thought to ask if I was expected to wear a uniform and was greatly relieved to find out, from Gayle when she finally arrived, that as office manager mine was the only non-uniformed position in the building. But I could have been spared some anxiety if Gayle had only thought to clarify this little item in advance of my arrival.

It is important to welcome newcomers to the organization. Why? Presumably the new hire brings something of value to the group and, if you want them to stay a while, it might be good to make them feel comfortable as they begin. Truthfully, there are few things in life more uncomfortable than the first day on a new job. To begin with you simply don't know where anything *is*. The essentials always come down to three things: the bathrooms, the break room, and the exits. Supply closets run a distant fourth. Everything else is just frosting on the cake of the new job. Even if you really wanted the new job (and let's face it, many of us have accepted a job at some desperate juncture in our lives that we didn't even *want*, but had to accept) most of us cannot help but dread the first day. In some respects it is worse than the first day in a new school; because there, at least, there will be a teacher in charge telling you where to go and what to do next. This is not necessarily the case on a new job.

There may or may not be someone in charge who will point you to the facilities before you desperately need them. In fact, you may ask to be excused only to find yourself helplessly wandering the corridors trying to find a door appropriately labeled to meet your need. And those break rooms can be diabolically located in a basement half a block away, reached only via a byzantine series of hallways and stairs. Seasoned coworkers may leave you to figure out this maze on your own.

If you do manage to locate the break room on that first day, you may not have time to eat anything since you spent so much time trying to find the place. Yes, this actually happened – to me.

As for exits, one might reasonably think that it would be a simple matter of leaving by the same door you used when you first arrived. But no. You likely arrived on that first day to present yourself at a front desk in a lobby area, and then you were quickly whisked off to another floor, or wing, or another building entirely, where you were instructed to begin your labors. Come quitting time, no one asked if you knew where you were and whether you knew how to get back to where you began the day. So you walked out the nearest exit and looked around only to realize you had no idea where you had parked your car. And, yes, this also happened – to me.

Years after my first day at the dental office, I was managing the new employee orientation program at a mid-sized company; and much of what we incorporated into that program was informed by that long-ago first day. Being the "new kid on the block", even if you have been on the planet too long to be considered a kid, is uncomfortable at best and can be awful in the absence of some kind of welcome from, well ... someone.

At West Coast Communications (WCC) we made it a practice to inform the receptionist, the evening before a new hire was to begin their employment, of the new person's name and assigned employee number. The receptionist could then prepare a temporary ID badge. Granted it was one of those flimsy paper things you slip into a plastic holder with a pin attached to the back of it, but at least the new person knew they were expected. That matters. This also allowed the receptionist to greet that individual by name and say something like, "Hi, Jane (or John), welcome to West Coast Communications. We are glad you are here." Clichéd? Perhaps. But even that can be welcome when you don't know what to expect.

In decades of welcoming new people to the workplace, I found there was no better way to help that person assimilate and learn the basics than to assign them a buddy for a few days. The buddy-system allowed the incoming employee to shadow someone during those first unnerving days. The newbie could also ask all the questions, one-on-one, they were too uncomfortable to ask in a group setting. I learned that the experienced "buddy" also gained some insight by serving in that role. He or she sometimes let me know that they gained new appreciation for the big picture of how the company operated, or they discovered the answer to some small mystery they had long wondered about.

Choosing the right person to act as the seasoned buddy is important. An overly confident show-off will bury the new person in non-essential trivia, just so they can display their expertise. Or if you select someone with a grudge against some department or group, it will color the new arrival's impression of that segment of the company. Buddy assignments should be reserved for those who know what they are doing, like their job, and know their way around the establishment. Such individuals are usually far too busy to be tasked with such a routine assignment and occasionally they told me so. I would then explain that this was actually a significant assignment (introducing a new talent into the organization) and I needed them to give it their best effort. Additionally, a gift card for lunch for two at a popular local eatery was usually well-received. Such appreciation expressed in advance, as an act of good faith, was usually rewarded by a job well done.

At the last company where I was in charge of welcoming newcomers, we eventually made new employee-orientation an all-day affair. It was conducted monthly, with coffee and pastries served in the morning to begin the day on a pleasant note, during an informal meet-and-greet setting. The agenda included practical information from various areas of the company (such as operations, customer service, sales and marketing, etc.) presented by a director who explained his or her particular area of responsibility and how it interfaced with the rest of the company. We also incorporated the company's philosophy on safety, and included some of the basic employee relations segments, such as our sexual harassment prevention policy. This was not training on these topics, that would come soon; but was rather an introduction to the fact that safety, respect, and courtesy were important, that we believed they mattered in our day-to-day work experience.

It was my privilege, as the head of HR, to open the day with a brief welcome and a quick overview of the history of the organization. We distributed a book that contained the story of how this nearly century-old company came to be and why we believed it was a good place to work. Thus we re-iterated the welcome they had received their first day, took time to answer their questions, and provided speakers who shared insights and stories about what is was like to work there. We then closed the day by telling them that we were glad they had decided to join us and we looked forward to working with them. Too often the organization emphasizes its own decision to hire someone, neglecting to acknowledge that the individual made a decision to join them. This decision making process needs to be a two-way street, not a one-way privilege.

An all-day "Welcome, we are glad you are here," served to convey that we genuinely valued their potential contributions and we wanted them to succeed. Not infrequently, an attendee would see me in the hallway or the break room days or even weeks later and comment, "You know that was the most helpful orientation I have ever attended. Thanks!"

That was enough to make me smile for at least the rest of the day. We all need a place to be, a way to contribute, and a sense that someone in that place cares about how we are getting along. Yes, a job is work; but it does not have to anonymous drudgery. It can become a place of belonging where we can achieve and thrive. That was the goal.

Tending Tip: Those new to the organization, even if they already possess good job skills, need some guidance as they find their place. A good start is simply to make sure they feel welcome. It can make a big difference in how they fit into the organization over the long-term.

Chapter Six

HOLES IN STOCKINGS AND STORIES

As I waited for the candidate to arrive, I once again reviewed her resume. It looked strong–Paula C. Devlin, R.N. She had a lot of experience and some impressive achievements over the years. I kept glancing out the window while I worked and, because my office happened have windows that faced the main parking lot of our building, I saw a woman I presumed to be Paula pull into a parking space as she arrived for the interview.

Oddly she did not immediately get out of her car. Instead she sat there, looking – I didn't quite know how she looked–but something was off. So I kept watching and then I saw her lift a small paper bag from the seat and put it to her mouth. She repeated this a couple of times and then checked her hair in the rear view mirror and touched up her lipstick. Then she slowly opened the car door and got out. However, she only made it a few steps toward the entrance when she stumbled and fell. Not a full face-plant, but a fall to her knees hard enough that she struggled to get back up. She straightened her skirt and then resumed her walk toward the front entrance, but with a very careful and measured gait. This was concerning and I suspected that this was going to be a brief interview.

My intercom buzzed as the front desk receptionist told me my candidate was in the lobby. I said, "Send her back," and rose to greet her as we shook hands and exchanged names and pleasantries. I invited Paula to have a seat at the conference table in my office as I brought her paperwork over from my desk and joined her.

She began by telling me about her lengthy experience in both hospitals and clinics. I was struggling to pay attention to what she was saying, however, because her slightly disheveled appearance belied her strong job qualifications. Her dress, which was not quite clean at the cuffs of her sleeves, did not look like it had seen an iron recently. As she spoke, some of her words were slightly, only very slightly, slurred. Although she rarely made eye contact, when she did her eyes were a little glassy.

Finally she noticed that I was not asking many questions, and she cast her eyes down at her hands, folding and unfolding them nervously in her lap. When she did this she suddenly noticed a big hole in both knees of her nylons (caused by her earlier fall) a sight I had been trying very hard to ignore. Immediately she began to apologize, explaining that she realized this must look bad, but that she had been in a hurry dressing for the interview, couldn't find a new pair of nylons, and thought her dress would cover the holes. She continued to spin out her story until I carefully interrupted her.

"Paula, I don't think that is quite what happened, is it? I should tell you that I saw you fall in the parking lot coming in."

One of the most difficult communication challenges, at least in my experience, is how to deal with someone who is blatantly lying to you. You can confront them and challenge their truthfulness, but that also means you are likely to get into a back and forth about their character. (And your own.) Calling someone a liar is seldom productive. It is usually more effective to stick to describing what you have seen and heard; thus I simply told Paula that I had seen her fall.

"Well, there was a bump in the pavement and my toe caught on it and ..." slowly she wound down unto silence. It was time to address the elephant in the room.

"Paula, I am very sorry, but I must ask you – have you been drinking today?"

"What? No. Why would you ask me something like that? I told you, I stumbled that's all." She attempted to deflect my scrutiny by saying how much she liked our offices. She said she could tell we were a well-run operation by the appearance of the office layout, and by how many nurses we had on duty in the call center. She had observed this during her long walk down the aisle between rows of cubicles occupied by nurses on the phone with clients. She continued more rapidly now, trying to get in as much of her pitch as she could, asserting her desire to contribute to the "goals of the organization" while also offering that she really needed this job. She had two daughters at home and was a single mom. She *really* needed this job, she stated. Finally, I called a halt to what was rapidly deteriorating into a charade of a job interview.

"Paula, I am very sorry to have to tell you that I am going to end this interview now. I appreciate you taking the time to meet with us, but I don't think there is any point in continuing."

She looked scared and flustered, as she blurted out, "Okay, so maybe I had a quick drink before I got here. You know how it is. Job interviews are nerve wracking and I just wanted to relax my nerves – a little. That's all."

Now I had another dilemma. She wasn't our employee, so I had no authority to ask her to call someone for a ride home. But neither could I, in good conscience, send her out into that parking lot, knowing she would drive off clearly under the influence.

"Paula, do you have anyone you can call to come and pick you up and take you home?"

She shook her head and began to cry.

"Do you live near a bus stop? There is a bus that goes right by our office here about every half an hour. Would that work? I could ask security to allow you to leave your car here until you could come back and get it."

Weeping she said "No. I came in from Elk Ridge and it is about thirty minutes from here."

Finally, after a quick call to the front desk to confirm there was enough petty cash on hand for a sizable cab fare, I explained that I did not want to cause her any further trouble, but for her own safety we were going to call a cab and pay for her ride home. Then I gave her the number of a help-line for substance abuse issues, which she could use without cost, and encouraged her to give them a call.

I have never experienced the kind of humiliation Paula must have experienced that afternoon. Although I had no desire to play the enabler, I did want to send her out with some glimmer of hope. Despair can become deadly. "Paula, if you decide to deal with your drinking, once you are back on track, we would be glad to accept your application and would consider you for an interview."

"Really?" she asked tearfully.

"Yes, really. I wish you better days ahead, Paula."

While I felt sorry for Paula, I was also thankful that she was not my problem. We had enough of those. Like nearly all employers in recent years, our workforce had its share of people with serious issues; some of whom had simply not yet been identified as being at work under the influence. With the advent of the Drug-Free Workplace Act (DFWA) of 1988, employers could not end someone's employment solely because an individual had a substance abuse problem, or in some cases, just because someone *suspected* he or she had an addiction problem. Such identification needed to be coupled with documentation regarding a specific lack of performance on the job. This was to make any decisions more objective than subjective.

So, for example, instead of a supervisor opining that "Bob lacks energy and I suspect he is drinking again" the employer needed to make a more objective case. "Bob has appeared distracted and unfocused on his work for the past two weeks. The result of this is that he was late for work three times and has missed two critical project deadlines." Thus we had a specific timeframe, an observed behavior, and a verifiable work/productivity impact.

Unless the person in question posed an immediate safety risk to themselves or others, usually there was a corrective process to go through. If, during that process, the employee declared they needed help and wanted to go into a treatment program, we were legally required to support them in getting the help they needed. This was a good thing in many cases. It was always preferable to retain good job skills and preserve institutional knowledge whenever possible. But there were inevitably those who tried to game the system by sheltering under the DFWA, while continuing their addictive behaviors. While they were actively in this denial phase all kinds of chaos could, and often did, ensue. And the damage was not limited to their own lack of productivity.

The negative impact upon their co-workers was detrimental to team morale resulting in even further loss of productivity. This continues to be a significant workplace problem, greater than many people realize. Some studies have suggested that on any given day 5% of the employee population is at work under the influence. This means that for every one thousand employees, there are likely fifty individuals impaired while at work. Lost productivity due to substance abuse issues in the workplace in the United States in 2018 was estimated to be about twenty-five billion dollars, according to author Jeffrey Juergens in a July, 2019, article written for AddictionCenter.com.[6]

Craig fell off a piece of heavy equipment and broke his leg while on duty. A member of his team, who later acknowledged that he was "sick and tired of watching Craig stumbled around" made a call to HR to suggest that we might want to drug-test Craig in light of his accident. Craig refused to take a post-accident drug test and it took the company nearly forty-eight hours to get a court order requiring one. Even two days after his accident, he still tested positive for several illegal drugs in his system. He continued lying about his drug use even after the tests results came back. As the cliché goes, denial is not just a river in Egypt.

Then there was Randy, who was found by a co-worker slumped semi-comatose over his computer keyboard with a morphine "lollipop" still dangling from his mouth. (Prior to this incident I had never heard of such a thing, but such lollipops were a type of slow-absorption narcotic used for pain relief.) Yes, he had a prescription for this medication due to an old, non-work-related, back injury. Still he could hardly perform his duties while unconscious. So he was written up and sent home. He then claimed DFWA protection and entered rehab.

A few weeks later he returned, shortly to pull the same stunt again. After much wrangling and documentation his employment was terminated. He showed no remorse, only irritability that he had been caught – again. He seemingly cared nothing about the disruption to his entire department when the EMTs had to come rushing through the office to put him on a gurney and load him into the ambulance. Not his problem, but it was definitely ours.

Entire cottage industries have sprung up around dealing with this issue. One assertively gung-ho company offered to provide drug-sniffing dogs to patrol our locker rooms, parking lots, and work sites. Their fees were reasonable and their references came straight from a local law enforcement agency. We gave it some thought and then declined their services.

As I had often declared to my own subordinates, and to any and all managers who wished my department to crack down on their offending employees, "We are the human *resources* department – *not* the HR police." How could we expect employees to come to us with their concerns and issues, if they saw us as some kind of para-law-enforcement agency? No. Was not happening, not if I could help it. So no, to the drug-sniffing dogs.

It is a good thing for anyone struggling with a substance abuse problem to have the opportunity to get help and, at the same time, be able to retain their employment rather than to be summarily fired. We all need a second chance at some time, for something. But the tsunami of substance abuse in our society has also created a drunken and drugged workforce, more often than many people realize. This in turn creates risks and hazards for both themselves and their co-workers and creates complex issues that must be addressed.

While tending people, you will sometimes be told heart rending stories, and be presented with wild assertions and surreal accounts of events – some of them may actually be true. But not infrequently, it will turn out that these stories have holes in them. Lots of holes. And it may fall to you, as the person charged with separating fact from fiction, to identify those holes and fill them with verifiable facts. That will often get you close to where you need to be. What facts alone will not do, however, is show you how to proceed with exposing the necessary truth, while refusing to indulge in unnecessary self-righteousness. It is possible to act with restraint toward the dishonest employee while not accepting or excusing their behavior. However, it is seldom easy. It is a hard task to poke holes in the story while avoiding putting a hole in the person. Or as Robert Greenleaf puts it in *On Becoming a Servant Leader*, it is important to be able to "*judge the erring action and not judge the essential person.*"[7]

Most HR professionals struggle with the dynamic tension involved between acting as a policy enforcer when required, rather than as a resource to support people in contributing their best work. Certainly HR professionals have a considerable amount of authority which we may use when appropriate. Personally, I never enjoyed telling other people what to do. And I truly hated "catching" someone doing the wrong thing. However, I did want to be able to come along side someone struggling to find their way in the workplace, and help them cut through their own hindrances and come out a success. It was always the goal, but not always the result.

Tending Tip:
- Perhaps the most useful balance on the accountability spectrum that we can hope to achieve is accomplished by holding the person accountable without handing down any personal judgement. We are there to assist the individual when possible, and administer policy where necessary; but we are not there to ascribe judgement.
- People-tending is more often effective when done with a scalpel than with a blunt instrument.

Chapter Seven

No Good Deed Goes Unpunished

Some people manage with efficiency, but little else. They tend to be arid leaders who meet deadlines, but inspire no particularly fine contributions from their team. Others manage through forming good relationships coupled with solid reliability. But few can manage a team of people with efficiency, good relationships, and reliability, while also demonstrating grace and good humor. Lonnita, however, was such a person.

She was a nurse with years of experience in clinical settings, who also excelled at managing a team of fellow nurses in a managed care unit of an HMO (health maintenance organization), which is a whole other skill set, and a much more complex one at that. It was to the organization's credit that it had recognized Lonnita's value and had promoted her to a director's position, where she excelled in delivering good care and service through her staff to hundreds of online patients each week. We were glad to have her with us. Her bright-eyed approach to problem solving and her smiling face were just an added bonus.

I was, therefore, completely unprepared when one afternoon the VP of managed care operations, Kathy, called me into her office to discuss Lonnita's upcoming annual performance evaluation. Although I often guided supervisors and managers in developing an evaluation of their subordinates, at this time in my career I did not usually weigh in on director level personnel. It was, to use a hackneyed phrase, above my pay grade.

Furthermore, I also reported directly to Kathy, and thus Lonnita was my peer. While 360-type evaluations (wherein the recipient receives feedback from superiors, peers and subordinates) were becoming more prevalent, they had not yet been adopted by our company. So I was mystified, particularly since Kathy had never before asked me to assist her with any of her own subordinates' evaluations. This was awkward. But I was floored when Kathy explained what she wanted me to do.

"I'm going to have you do some background work for me this year, in developing Lonnita's performance evaluation," Kathy said. "I want you to go through her case reports, her monthly statistical data, and her evaluations of her own subordinates. I am going to be giving her a Level 2 performance rating and I don't have time to look up all the data for substantiating that, so I need you to prepare it for me. Have it ready by day after tomorrow. I'm traveling tomorrow and won't be back until the next day."

We used a standard five level evaluation format: 1- Unacceptable performance, 2- Performance Improvement Needed, 3 – Performance Satisfactory, 4- Above Standard Performance, and 5 – Outstanding Performance. This kind of appraisal is what is commonly called a Likert-type scale, named after Rensis Likert, the psychologist who first developed it in 1932.[8]

Generally speaking, fewer than 10% of any employee population received a Level 1 rating during any given year and, unless they had shown substantial improvement, those who did were often let go within six months after receiving such a rating. A Level 2, while obviously not quite so dire, was usually reserved for serious lack of performance and often resulted in being placed on some kind of Performance Improvement Plan (PIP). It also usually meant the Level 2 employee would not be eligible for any kind of pay raise that year.

Dumbfounded, I stuttered out a feeble question. "You are talking about Lonnita, right?"

Kathy gave me a frosty stare and replied, "You heard me. Have the information compiled when I return. And obviously don't discuss this with anyone since, as you well know, all evaluations are confidential. That's all." I was dismissed.

Returning to my own office at the opposite end of the suite, I sat down heavily, put my elbows on my desk, and dropped my head into my hands. Good grief, how had this come about? What in the world was going on? I was flummoxed. Nevertheless, as the afternoon wore on, I began to pull files, dig through statistical data, and generally gnaw through my own anxiety. As expected, Lonnita's reports were thorough but concise. Her data was accurate and complete as far as I could determine. Her evaluations of her own subordinates were fair, and responses to those evaluations in the employee comment section reflected their appreciation of her leadership. Criticism was constructive and specific, just what you would hope for from an accomplished professional.

I next looked for "recency bias" – meaning she tended to rate an employee disproportionately higher, because of a single incident of outstanding performance just prior to the evaluation, or conversely lower, due to a significant failure shortly before the evaluation was due. None that I could see. Did she play favorites? Was she unduly harsh toward any specific team member? None of the common errors in appraisal development jumped out at me. So I did what I often did when I could think of no other way to present the information without inserting some personal bias of my own. I created a graph showing how many appraisals she had delivered during the annual rating period, what the curve looked like as to rating spread, and how it compared to the prior year's evaluation data.

The next day I examined Lonnita's case management reports, specifically looking to see whether there had been a significant increase in patient complaints or in undesirable patient outcomes. Neither emerged. Finally, I wrote up a one-page summary outlining Lonnita's departmental goals and team performance for the period in question. There was nothing that I had been able to identify that would seem to warrant a Level 2 rating. It might not be a Level 5, but it looked like a solid Level 4 to me. My experience caused me to believe that I had a sound basis for my judgment on this as I reviewed dozens of evaluations each year for other managers.

Then I put the whole thing away and went to do some work with one of my own teams. It was always a balancing act, and a common one among nearly all the managers I knew, this business of managing upward to your boss's expectations, and managing downward with your own team to meet the organization's goals. I was dreading my meeting with Kathy slated for the following day.

Kathy buzzed me just before 4:00 p.m. the day she returned and I trudged down the long aisle between the rows of cubicles to her office. This was not going to be pretty. I had done as instructed, but the result was not going to be to her liking. That was problematic enough; but what I could not figure out was the "why" of it. What had occurred that had caused Kathy to decide to rate Lonnita so poorly? During my deep-dive the past couple of days, I had learned that Lonnita had never received anything other than Level 4 or 5 evaluations in the seven or eight years she had been with the company.

The two women were complete opposites in many ways. Kathy, who was a striking blonde, was about ten years younger than Lonnita, even though she was Lonnita's boss. Kathy had been with the company fewer years than Lonnita, but had risen rapidly through the ranks before being promoted to VP of the region just before I joined the company. Lonnita was a lovely, dark-haired, Hispanic woman who nearly always exhibited a cheerful and calm demeanor; whereas Kathy tended to be somewhat volatile in her leadership style.

After taking a seat, I handed Kathy the report I had prepared. She quickly perused the one-page summary, gave me a sharp glance and continued on to the body of the report itself. After another few minutes she slapped the whole thing onto her glass-topped desk and said, "This isn't what I was looking for, Marsha. Lonnita *is* getting a Level 2 eval, and you were supposed to supply the substantiating data to validate that. You did understand that, didn't you?"

"I did understand what you were hoping for. I simply couldn't locate anything that met that criteria," I responded.

"Well, this isn't acceptable. I'll give you one more chance to get this right. Go back and find me the information I am looking for. Period. Or we are going to be having a conversation of a different kind altogether. Am I clear?"

I simply nodded and left. Still not understanding what was going on, I decided that maybe I had taken a wrong approach. My deep-dive had, perhaps, been too granular. I would step back and try to take a look from the thirty-thousand foot level. Try to figure out the big picture. So I spent a few hours looking at every major project Lonnita and her group had been tasked with over the past year. I looked at the deadlines associated with each of them, and then following a couple of urgent requests to accounting, I examined whether the projects had been completed within budget. Every project had been delivered on time (a couple were actually a week or two early) and, with one minor exception, each had been completed within the assigned budget.

As fate would have it, there was just one other office between my own office and Lonnita's. So I passed her open office door multiple times each day in the course of my other duties. I tried to avoid getting into any meaningful conversations with her during those two days, lest I allow my anxiety to cause me to let something slip. I liked and respected Lonnita and I was determined to maintain a friendly posture, despite the pressure I was under from our boss. She seemed unaware of any trouble brewing and it was not my place to inform her of such, not to mention that I had been specifically forbidden to do so.

Being in close proximity to someone about whom you have potentially "job-threatening" knowledge, which you cannot disclose, is one of the more difficult aspects of working in HR. What you know and what you can say are often light-years apart. The ability to maintain confidentiality, even when you personally disagree with what is transpiring, is one hallmark of a seasoned professional. Those who find it too awkward and pressure-laden generally do not remain in HR for very long. And the HR person who breaks confidentiality usually finds themselves unemployed very quickly.

That evening at home, sitting pensively with a hot cup of tea, I considered my options. There weren't many. Of course, it would be possible to deliberately skew the data to make Lonnita look less successful than she was. But I had never done a thing like that in my life and I was not about to start now. Lonnita did not deserve it and I was not going to be a party to it. I could wait to see what Kathy's reaction was, once she looked at the further data I would be giving her the next day. However, she had already made it plain that it likely would be ugly.

That left only one alternative that I could think of. I could take a proactive stance. I have never liked being cast as someone else's puppet or a victim of circumstances. But I was also human and unemployment was not appealing either. Still, as M. Scott Peck once wrote, "*In order to be free to do the unpopular, upon occasion, the ... manager must be prepared to quit her position or be fired at any moment.*" So I prayed, asking for strength to resign if necessary, and to be able to do it without equivocation or drama. No one had ever warned me that being in human resources might one day mean being all-too-human while protecting fellow "human resources" who did not know they were in any difficulty.

The next morning, Kathy called me earlier than she usually did. I presented the newly developed over-view of Lonnita's performance, showing she had met both every deadline given to her and had, with that one small exception, done so within the budgetary guidelines. I had read and heard the phrase, "steam coming out of someone's ears" many times. This was the first time I had ever come close to actually seeing such a thing. Kathy looked like the top of her head might explode.

"You do know this isn't *at all* what I asked for?" she asked rhetorically.

"Kathy, I do know that. And I don't take it lightly that you are my boss and that I am obligated to follow your instructions. But I also know Lonnita and I have worked alongside her this past year. There is nothing in her file, her reports, or her behavior, that I can identify that warrants her receiving a Level 2 evaluation. It simply isn't there. And it is clear that you are angry with me."

"Oh, that doesn't even begin to cover it. You know I could consider this flagrant insubordination on your part," Kathy stated, leaving no room for misunderstanding.

"Yes, I get that. So I just don't see any other way to handle this except to offer my resignation. If that is what you decide you want, please let me know by the end of the day and I will have my letter of resignation on your desk by 8:00 a.m. tomorrow morning." Apparently she did not see that one coming, as I had never seen anyone both glare and gape at the same time. But she did. I left while I could still put one foot in front of the other.

When I got back to my office, I put in a call to national headquarters in the Midwest to Jim, the Sr. VP of HR, whom I had never met in person, but with whom I had a matrix reporting relationship. Operationally on the local front I reported directly to Kathy, but when it came to complex or highly charged specific HR issues, Jim was my direct up line for those matters. His depth of expertise in the HR field was well known within the profession, extending even beyond our own large organization of more than ten thousand employees.

We had had a number of friendly and productive phone conversations over the prior two years, wherein Jim had given me some expert guidance. As the head of HR for thousands of employees nationwide, he usually worked in strategic workforce planning and direction. As a regional HR manager, overseeing a few hundred employees, I was very small fry by comparison and I had no idea how he would react to what I was about to tell him. However, since it appeared that this issue was going to cost me my job, I saw no reason why it should also cost Lonnita her job. And if Kathy hamstrung Lonnita with a poor performance rating, despite her fine work, it seemed highly likely that for some unknown reason, Kathy was positioning Lonnita for termination before much longer.

"Hello, Jim. This is Marsha out in Western Region and I am calling to let you know that I have just offered Kathy my resignation. I thought perhaps you should be aware of why I did that."

Fast forward two months. It turned out Jim had received more than one report from Western Region, unbeknown to me, regarding Kathy's management tactics. Some were in writing and signed by the sender, while others were anonymous phone calls. Among them were not a few accounts of abuse of power and retaliation. It was further revealed that a couple of years earlier, just before I joined the company, Kathy had been out on a personal leave for several weeks during which time Lonnita filled in as the acting head of the region. Lonnita had done such a good job that Kathy received multiple reports praising Lonnita from colleagues far and wide, even from headquarters. Kathy was furious.

Instead of being grateful that her colleague had kept the ship sailing smoothly in her absence, Kathy resented being "shown up". She had waited two long years to punish Lonnita simply for doing a good job. I was to have been Kathy's cudgel or plain old dupe. But it backfired on her – big time.

Kathy did not accept my offer of resignation and I never learned why. And failing to find any substantiation for a sub-standard eval, she had settled for giving Lonnita a Level 3 acceptable rating. But meanwhile, on a seemingly ordinary Thursday morning two months later, two executives flew in unannounced from headquarters and confronted Kathy with her misdeeds. They gave her forty-five minutes to clean out her desk and box up her personal belongings, before they escorted her from the building. She was a VP and the employees were agog as Kathy's termination of employment transpired … or so I was told a few days later.

I was not present when it happened. I was sitting in a hospital waiting room about one hundred miles away when this all took place. During the weeks preceding Kathy's dismissal, headquarters had asked me to work with them, under the strictest confidentiality, to compile data and reports to lay the groundwork for her termination. But during that crushingly toxic two months, between when I refused to throw Lonnita under the bus and when national HR appeared on our doorstep, Kathy had been on the warpath. She had done everything she could to make my life miserable, including stripping me of nearly all working authority and re-assigning my teams to other managers. I was left isolated and, by every appearance to my colleagues, humiliated for reasons unknown to them. I suspected they thought Kathy was preparing to fire me and I could say nothing to explain.

In midst of all of this, the week before Kathy's dismissal, I received a call from yet another HR executive from headquarters, Carol, a member of Jim's staff.. She informed me that she was in town and would like to meet with me after regular office hours, at the hotel where she was staying. The offsite meeting was because the company did not want anyone on the staff to get wind of what was coming before they pulled the rip cord. It felt a little like being in a spy novel the evening I walked into the hotel restaurant to meet her.

Carol informed me of the upcoming date they had targeted for Kathy's dismissal, and I told her that I was already scheduled to be out of the office for a few days during that time, due to an immediate family member's very serious surgery. I added that this had been on the calendar for several weeks. Carol asked me a couple of questions about the surgery and when she learned the basic circumstances she was visibly unsettled.

"Do you mean to tell me that while you have been dealing with this chaotic disaster at the office, you have also been dealing with this medical issue in your own family?" she asked somewhat incredulously. I replied, "Yes, sometimes life bunches up on you." Carol just shook her head and then told me that she was sorry that I had had to endure Kathy's wrath during these recent months. She also pledged the continuing full support of the company's HR department. Finally, I could see a light at the end of this long dark tunnel. Thus, when the day of Kathy's dismissal from the company arrived, I was sitting in a hospital waiting room with much more serious matters on my mind.

A few weeks later, I had a new boss, Jane C., who as it turned out, actually liked working with me. I was both relieved and grateful. Within Jane's first few months in the region, she reorganized the regional structure and promoted me. In addition to regaining many of my old team members, I was given an expanded scope of responsibility and authority. Headquarters let me know they appreciated that I had been what they deemed a "calm and steady influence" during the recent turbulent months. (Little did they know how unsteady I had often felt during that period of time.)

Regardless, I was not sure whether the outcome was really worth all the sleepless nights, not to mention the Mylanta antacid I had chugged straight from the bottle while at my desk, during those awful weeks. Although I hoped I would never have to go through something like this again, I never forgot Peck's admonition, to be prepared to do the unpopular if necessary and right, and to also be prepared to face the consequences.

Tending Tip: It is easy to get caught up in the dramatics sometimes displayed in the workplace. The lure of palace intrigue can be seductive and the temptation to choose up sides, or worse, to descend into the pit of manipulation can be powerful. I encourage you to be wary of the law of unintended consequences when faced with hidden personal agendas on the job. I can almost guarantee that you will never regret avoiding them whenever possible.

"All shall be well, and all shall be well, and all manner of thing shall be well." – Julian of Norwich [10]

Chapter Eight

GREASE PITS AND POWER PLAYS

The day Howard came to my office, it was not his uniform or his job title that caught my full attention; no, it was the look of honest anger in his eyes. It was the expression of a man who had had enough. I did not know it then, but this first-level supervisor was eventually going to put me on a collision course with the most powerful man in the company, the CEO.

Howard was a proud man, although he did not at first appear to be one. His work clothes were ordinary, made of the kind of sturdy navy or khaki material found in the uniforms of many companies, worn by mostly men who did the hard manual labor of the enterprise. His daily responsibilities were relatively straight forward. He supervised employees who changed the oil, rotated the tires, checked the transmissions, and performed a dozen other detailed tasks to maintain the company vehicles. He and his crew tended to duties that were lowly in nature; but they did them well and with a sense of pride in their work.

These mechanics and technicians did not attend meetings where multi-million dollar budgets were debated. But they made sure the air pressure was correct on all four tires of the sedans driven to such meetings by managerial types. The fact was that the fleet of over two hundred vehicles was a much larger line item in the annual budget than that of the entire department over which some of these polished executives presided. Sometimes, the workers at the bottom of an organization bear a much greater responsibility for the financial health of the organization than those nearer the top ever realize.

"Come in, Howard, and have a seat. It's nice to meet you. What can I do for you today? Your voice mail only said that you had an urgent matter you would like to discuss, but nothing more."

Howard sat down, but nothing about him suggested he was relaxed. His spine was ramrod straight and his expression was grim.

"I've only been to HR once before, and it was years ago. It wasn't a pleasant experience, either. But I have heard in the last couple of years that things had changed over here. So I first need to ask you, is what we discuss today confidential?"

I assured him that it was, unless I heard anything from him that placed me in a position where I would have a legal obligation to report the matter – things like worker safety, potential violence, or provable theft.

Howard got an odd look on his face and said that what he wanted to talk to me about didn't fall into any of those categories, as far as he knew.

We spent the next several minutes getting acquainted. He had been with the company for over a decade, and except for one incident more than five years earlier, he had a clean work history. That incident, he candidly admitted, had been his fault and had happened during a time when he was going through a divorce and was drinking too much. He had not been drinking at work, but he had come to work with a hangover and had gotten into a heated argument with a co-worker. He had received a written disciplinary action and a one-day suspension without pay.

I assured him that as far as I was concerned anything that had only happened once, and at that more than five years ago, was ancient history and would not have any bearing upon my handling of whatever the current issue might be. Howard took a deep breath and seemed to relax just a little.

"Then I need to report something and I am not sure exactly how to do that, or even whether you can do anything about it. But rather than just quit and walk away, I feel like I owe it to my team and others in our unit to at least try to see if we can get things fixed in our department. It is a miserable place to work, and my men deserve better than they have been getting from our manager."

I asked and was told the name of his manager, Bill G., whom I had never met. I then asked Howard to tell me, in as much detail as he was comfortable with, exactly what the problem was. The next forty-five minutes were a litany of incidents of petty meanness, nasty gamesmanship, and a general tale of workplace woe the likes of which I had seldom, if ever, heard. It was disgusting and disheartening. When Howard finally ran out of steam, I asked why he had waited so long to report this behavior. I told him that I realized it isn't easy to lodge a complaint about your own manager, that can be risky, but I added, "You don't seem like someone who is easily intimated."

"So what took so long?" I asked quietly. I had a feeling that there was another shoe yet to be dropped. Still, there was no way I could have anticipated the next fact he laid at my office doorstep like a dead rat.

"Bill" he said dryly, "is a personal friend of the CEO."

I was a little confused. Howard's boss, Bill G., was a lower-level manager with a limited education and no particularly valuable job skills. He had only held one other job, in general vehicle maintenance, before coming to our company as a mechanic and eventually rising to manager of fleet maintenance. But he had been here for twenty-five years, longer, in fact, than the CEO.

The CEO, Marvin, on the other hand, had an undergraduate degree from a good university, followed by a master's degree in finance. Marvin had worked for a top 100 company in the Fortune 500 before coming to work here, first as an outside consultant, then as an executive and finally as CEO. What could the two possibly have in common?

Howard explained that Bill had made it a point to ingratiate himself with Marvin when he had first arrived, and eventually had made himself into a kind of general go-to guy in those earlier years. Once Marvin had become CEO, although they no longer worked in the same location, they still had lunch together every few weeks. Bill took advantage of these working lunches to undermine anyone he disliked. It had become well-recognized throughout the organization that you did not want to get on the CEO's radar by way of one of Bill's lunch chats, not if you wanted your career to be long or prosperous.

"It came to a head this past couple of weeks," Howard continued, "over two different things. First Janet's mother got sick." He went on to explain that Janet was the departmental clerk and her mother had not been well for a long time, but then she got really sick and was hospitalized. Janet's mother lived in a neighboring state, several hours away by car.

"So Janet put in an emergency request for a few days off to go see her mom. Janet runs all the reports for our department showing how much we have saved the company in replacement parts, outside fees, things like that. The reports are due each quarter. That report was due to Bill the same week Janet requested the days off, so he denied her request. She told him it was a family emergency; but he said she could leave only after the report was delivered, in two days' time.

She couldn't get the report done any sooner because several guys have to give her their specific numbers for the quarter before she can do the departmental roll-up. Janet almost always has to work late the day the quarterly report is due. So she asked Bill again if she could postpone the report, just this once, until after she got back. He said no. So she worked till about seven that evening, drove four hours straight to get to the hospital, and was told when she arrived that her mom had died two hours earlier. I wanted to go punch his lights out when I heard that. She didn't get to say goodbye to her mom, because of that jerk's ego."

I sat there heartsick as I listened to Howard's account. He wasn't finished.

"Then last week, Scoop, one of our auto techs, was working the evening shift. I was still there as I was working late that evening. It was pouring rain, and I wasn't looking forward to going out in the wet and cold. I heard Scoop coughing and hacking away in the other room, next to the service bay. He's had a bad cough for about a week, but didn't want to use any of his sick days because Bill gets p———-d, uh sorry, Bill gets ticked-off anytime someone calls in sick.

Then I hear Bill out there, getting ready to leave to go to a big swanky dinner for some of the managers at his wife's company. He walks out into the service bay area and asks where his company car is, just as one of the guys is pulling it around from the parking lot. All three bays had vehicles in them, so Art had to leave Bill's car outside in the rain, pulled up as close as he could to the door. It was pouring.

Bill heard Scoop coughing and turned around and handed him his briefcase and his umbrella and told him, 'Here, walk me around to my car door, and hold my umbrella to make sure I don't get wet. This is a new suit and I've got a dinner to attend. And don't let my briefcase get wet either. That's Italian leather, you moron.'"

Scoop just looked at him and then took the umbrella and walked him around to open his car door, carrying Bill's brief case. Bill stayed dry while Scoop got soaked. And I mean drenched. Then Bill revved his engine and took off, splashing more water all over Scoop's pants and shoes. I told him to go into my office and try to get dry before he went back to the service bay.

Can a manager do that? Is that allowed, to just treat people like some kind of lackeys or servants, just because you are their boss?"

Now I was the one who needed to take a deep breath, because I knew we were going to be wading through some pretty deep water ourselves before this was all over.

Abuse of power by a manager toward his or her subordinates is one of the hardest things there is to call out to upper management. It is difficult for many reasons; but two are directly related to the nature of a tiered workforce. First, abuse can take so many forms that it can be a challenge to define exactly what it is and isn't. Secondly, abuse is often disguised as "joking around", hazing the new guy/girl, or even as exercising legitimate authority. Rarely will a boss actually say, "I'm the boss and I am doing this because I can and I don't give a rat's ___ what you think about it. So just do it."

They don't say it, but some think it, and some actually behave as though it is their God-given right to rule over their very own little jerkdom. Abuse of power in the work place has led to more heart attacks, stress related illnesses and lack of productivity than we will ever know about.

I thanked Howard for his time and told him that I would begin to look into this immediately. I also let him know that this would mean that I would have to conduct confidential interviews with a number of his co-workers, and that during this time, it would be better for all concerned if he did not discuss this complaint process with them.

As I routinely did, I also gave Howard my boss's number and said, "Howard, if at any time during or after this investigation you have questions or concerns about how I am handling this matter, I want you to feel free to call, Helen, my boss, and let her know about it. I am accountable here just like everyone else, and I want you to know that."

Howard looked at me with some surprise and also with a dawning new respect. I next outlined the approximate time table for how long it might take to conduct the necessary interviews, and I assured him that if there were any signs of retaliation against him for having reported his concerns, he should call me immediately.

I had no idea how convoluted and difficult the following weeks would become. (Continued in the next chapter.)

Tending Tip: Although we know that "might makes right" is a faulty premise, we do well to avoid assuming that "right makes might". Doing the right thing can sometimes involve taking a real risk and making yourself vulnerable, with no guarantee of the outcome.

Chapter Nine

INTO THE GREASE PIT

The next two weeks were challenging as I listened, day after day, to one account after another of Bill G.'s dictatorial approach to managing his department. I looked at his turnover rate and was not surprised to learn that it was approximately double the company average. As I read the personnel files of Bill's staff, I saw a steady stream of written warnings from him on nearly every department member about small infractions such as tardiness (some by as few as five minutes), tools not polished to perfection, and the like. The general picture that was evolving was that of a petty tyrant at the height of his powers. He not only enforced every company policy to the letter, he had layered on a few of his own making, such that his employees not only had to toe the line, his staff had to paint, polish, and dust the line on a weekly basis. This became even more painfully apparent when it was time to interview Janet.

She appeared at my office door, a quiet, somewhat mousy little woman in her mid-forties, dressed like someone twenty years older. Her slumped shoulders gave no indication of confidence, and her glance darted around like she was expecting to be disciplined at any moment. After we exchanged introductions, I explained to Janet that I was looking into some concerns that had been brought to my attention about the way her department was operating. Janet mumbled that she had heard something to that effect, but didn't know what she could contribute to the issue.

Gently I said, "Janet, I understand that your mother recently passed away. I am very sorry for your loss. Could you tell me about the circumstances of her illness and your request for a leave of absence related to it?"

Suddenly Janet bristled, just a little, beneath her wilted exterior. Her expression firmed up and her eyes hardened.

"That's personal. What's that got to do with anything?" she asked defensively. "I didn't make any complaints."

I told her that I realized she had not complained about it, but I wanted to confirm with her that her request to take a few days off, just prior to her mother's death, had been denied.

"Well, that's true. But Bill was within his rights to do that. I was making a request that was outside of department rules."

"I see. And what are the departmental rules about taking time off? I am familiar with what the company handbook states, but I don't think I am aware of your departmental rules."

Janet explained to me that in their department, it was required that you give thirty days' advance notice of any request for time off of more than one day. A single day off, required a week's advance notice. (The company policy required two weeks' notice for multiple days off, except in an emergency, and 24-hour notice for a day off.) She explained that she had only had a couple of days' notice from the hospital that her mother's condition was deteriorating and that although she had immediately put in for the days off, because she was requesting several days off, it did fall within the department's 30-day requirement.

"Janet, when your request was denied, did you go to anyone else, to see if an exception could be made?"

She looked at me like I had surely lost my mind. "No one goes around Bill. Not if you want to keep your job," she said bluntly.

She went on to add that she was a single woman with a household to support, including a son, who was attending the local community college, she added with no small tinge of maternal pride. She could not afford to put her job at risk.

After conducting approximately ten interviews, all of which corroborated Howard's initial concerns, I called our attorneys. We reviewed the facts as laid out by multiple witnesses, talked about the overall impact of such abusive management, and then got down to the bottom line. Was Bill creating liability for the company, and if so how much and how urgently?

Chad, the attorney with whom I worked most closely, was succinct and terse. "The answer to that question is easy. Bill is creating more liability than the company will want to deal with, and now that we have verified knowledge of it, the urgency is greater every single day that we do not deal with it. "

I told him about Bill's personal friendship with the CEO and asked for his input on how we should proceed. After a brief discussion, we agreed that I would have a conversation with the CEO first. If that did not go well, then Chad would weigh in.

I had only been with the company about a year and a half, and although my duties did not usually put me in the same meetings with the CEO, it happened that my office (largely glass-walled) was in close proximity to his. If an employee was just stopping by to talk, all blinds were open as was my office door. If their issue was private, but not terribly sensitive, then the door was closed, but the blinds were still open. If the matter was both private and sensitive, then I closed both the blinds and the door. During my interviews regarding Howard's complaint, there had been a lot of closed-blinds meetings in my office.

It was an uncomfortably obvious arrangement, and in later years my office was in a different building from most of the other executives. Furthermore, if an interview involved safety issues of a divisive nature, or complaints regarding upper management which could cause the person being interviewed to feel vulnerable, I had a small private conference room tucked away in an unobtrusive corner where the employee could come and go unobserved by fellow employees. But that was in the future and these were early days. Thus, unbeknown to me, the CEO had been taking note of the individuals who had been coming and going from my office, with closed-blind meetings often occurring.

The evening before our meeting I spent a considerable amount of time preparing. I had copies of each interview written up, a timeline of the investigation process, and a one-page summary of the complaint basis, the potential company policies that had been violated, and my recommendations (based upon legal counsel) about the response the company should undertake. It was not going to be an easy discussion.

Because it *was* the CEO, and in light of my relatively brief tenure with the company, combined with the fact that the complaint was directed at a personal friend of his, I had met with both my manager and her director the day before to review my findings and Chad's input on the legal implications. I had also asked whether either, or both, of them (my boss and her boss) would like to be present during my meeting with the CEO. Matters were further complicated by the fact that my manager's director (my boss's boss) was *also* a close personal friend of the CEO. I felt as if I were walking through a minefield in every direction. They told me it looked like I had conducted a solid investigation, and no, they did not feel the need to be present for the meeting.

Given that he was understandably a busy man, Marvin, the CEO, had required that our meeting occur prior to regular business hours. Thus, we met in his expansive office at 7:30 a.m. the next morning. His desk was half-a-football-field size, clearly meant to impress if not outright intimidate. His chairs were also large and covered in expensive leather. Since I am not very tall, I found myself perched uncomfortably near the edge of my seat, in order to assure that my feet actually touched the floor. The leather was slick and I could envision myself sliding right off the chair and onto the floor, if I wasn't careful.

I was carrying a large file folder with the back-up documents of the interviews, etc. Ordinarily a meeting involving multiple documents to be reviewed would be conducted at the conference table just off to the right of his desk area. It would have been much more convenient to be able to lay out the paperwork, as we talked. I also noticed that the chairs around his conference table were smaller than the two oversized, over-stuffed, leather club chairs placed before his desk. However, I was not invited to use either the conference table or the smaller, more comfortable chairs. His superiority in the meeting was made clear from the outset and the furniture and seating arrangements were only props to enhance his positional power in this little tableau. Making it clear that he was in charge, he opened the meeting.

"Good morning, Marsha. I understand you have some concerns you want to go over with me. I've noticed that you have had quite a few of

Bill G.'s people in and out of your office over the past couple of weeks. What's that all about?"

I swallowed hard, and said with as much professionalism as I could muster, "Yes. I have had several meetings recently with Bill's staff. Those meetings were the result of some issues that have been brought to my attention regarding his management style. May I ask, how familiar are you with Bill and his department?"

I had learned that it was better not to announce, out the gate, that the object of a complaint had been discovered to be a jerk and petty tyrant. This was particularly true when there was a relationship between the person with whom I was meeting and the alleged "jerk." So I tried to ease into the merge lane.

"I have known Bill for years. His department runs like a top. Never have had any complaints about him or his staff that I know of. Why, what seems to be the problem?" Marvin asked in a clipped manner.

"Well, one of the indicators that there is a problem is their turnover rate. It is approximately double that of any other department in the company. Were you aware of this?"

"No, I wasn't."

"I can understand that. You have much bigger fish to fry. And frankly, it would not be of any serious concern, other than from a dollars and sense perspective, if the turnover was basically reflective of only his entry-level personnel. They are fairly easy to replace. But three of the people who have left in the past year were ASE (Automotive Service Engineers) certified technicians with years of experience in fleet maintenance, and they are very scarce in this job market. We have had a recruitment open for one of those jobs for over three months now."

"Let's back up a minute," he said quickly. "What do you mean, from a 'dollars and sense perspective'? Aren't we saving money whenever a position is open? I realize it may cause some inconvenience to the other people in that area, but you sound like the turnover is actually costing us money."

I was always a little discomfited when men who knew the ins and outs of mergers and acquisitions, leveraged buy-outs, and stock options, were unaware of the basics of personnel costs and opportunities. But, that was generally considered to be "HR stuff" and nothing they really needed to worry about. Nevertheless, this was good ground we were on, because it was impersonal and data based, and in my experience, the favorite kind of discussion fodder for most executives. I had deliberately raised the turnover point first, in order to steer the discussion from an organizational efficiency perspective. We would get to Bill's peccadillos in due time.

"No, we are not saving money with these open positions, for two reasons. First, the remaining technicians we do have are putting in considerable overtime, at time and a half and occasionally even double time (because state law requires that anything over ten hours per day is paid at double the normal rate) in order to get the work done. We must either allow the over time or miss deadlines, or skip some routine maintenance, neither of which is preferable for the vehicles our men take into the field in safety-sensitive positions. CAL-OSHA (California Office of Safety and Health Administration) would frown on that."

He seemed surprised that I was familiar with the business nuts and bolts of the matter. Many executives assumed that HR was all about touchy-feely stuff, which made their skin crawl.

"Okay. What is the other reason?"

Without getting too far into the weeds, I quickly apprised Marvin of the costs, as validated by numerous national studies, of recruitment, training, and ramp-up time to replace certified technicians. It easily ran to the equivalent of six months to a year's wages for each position. Sometimes more.

"All right. So turnover in Bill's shop is an issue. What seems to be behind it?"

Now that I had established some hard data credibility with him, he seemed more willing to explore under lying causes, and that, as one of my legal beagle friends would say was "better than jacks for openers."

"First, I want to let you know that we are not talking about an isolated incident, or a whiner who just wants something to gripe about. I have spoken with a number of Bill's employees and there is consensus on the issues."

"And have you asked Bill for his side of the story?" Marvin asked with a decided edge to his tone.

Now it was my turn to be surprised. I had, as a matter of both fairness and routine procedure, interviewed Bill two days earlier. In HR we always interviewed the person about whom complaints were made, and we gave their version of events all the credit that was warranted. Not surprisingly, given what I had heard by the time Bill and I met, Bill was sarcastic, dismissive and rude during most of our interview. It was not until I gave him the routine final admonition before the meeting ended that he seemed to realize this could be serious for him.

"Bill, I need to let you know before you leave that we are taking the time and trouble to weigh every piece of information from as many angles as we can, before we decide what to do about all this. I understand that you disagree with the others and with their version of events. And that is your right.

However, what you need to understand is that they were simply exercising their right to make their concerns known to the company when they came to me. Those rights are protected by law and fully respected by this organization. In light of that, I can only respectfully caution you not to do or say anything, toward anyone you think may have been interviewed, that could be viewed by them or by a third party as retaliation.

A complaint is one thing," I continued in a matter-of-fact voice, "and it may or may not be validated; but retaliation is a whole other animal, and it almost always cuts both ways and everyone loses. I am not suggesting that you would purposely engage in any kind of retaliatory behavior. It is simply prudent that I advise you about how serious the consequences can be for anyone–you, me or anyone else–who takes that route."

Bill had gruffly acknowledged what I had said, but his complexion had paled a little as he left my office. He was beginning to realize that maybe, just maybe, he didn't hold all the cards in this particular game.

So now, two days later, it was my turn to be a little surprised. I had suspected that Bill's first phone call after our meeting would be to his lunch pal, the CEO. Apparently not. Marvin seemed unaware of whether or not I had met with Bill.

"Yes, I did interview Bill the day before yesterday. We reviewed, in detail, each and every aspect of the complaints about his management style. I gave him dates, times, and specific issues. Where appropriate, or unavoidable, I also gave him the name of the person making the allegation."

The CEO thought for a moment and then asked, "And how did he respond? Knowing Bill, I would guess he was not very happy about all this. Of course, who would be?"

This was the first time Marvin had acknowledged that he knew Bill personally. From here on, I was going to have to tread as lightly as I could.

"He was, as you suspected, pretty unhappy about the whole matter. Would you like to know of a couple of the specifics of the complaints about Bill's management style?"

"Do I have a choice?" Marvin said.

"Yes, you do. We could just go directly to the one-page summary that covers the basic complaint, policy and or legal violations, and company response, if you prefer. But since, as you say, you do know Bill, I thought you might want to know something of the specifics involved before we go to the bottom line."

Then, without waiting for his consent, I took a quick breath and recounted the death of Janet's mother after her request for leave was denied, and the case of Scoop standing in the rain covering Bill with his umbrella, when Scoop was already sick, and too afraid to take one of his earned sick days.

Marvin looked first skeptical, then nonplussed and finally taken aback. "This is not just water-cooler gossip? This is verifiable?" he asked.

"It has already been verified, by multiple witnesses, who were personally present when these incidents took place. And I have copies of Janet's leave request form and Bill's denial response to it. I have the doctor's note saying Scoop had walking pneumonia and eventually ended up missing a whole week of work because of it, just days after the umbrella incident. And lastly, sir, as hard as this is to tell you, these are just the tip of the ice berg. I could quickly list six or seven similar accounts. But that isn't necessary, is it? You are the CEO and you know how problematic this is for the company."

There was nearly a full minute of silence in that cavernous office. That is a long time to sit on the edge of a slick chair that is too big for you, and hold your tongue, which in my case is sometimes too sharp for my own good. But I had been at this kind of thing for a while and I knew when to stop talking.

"So what is your recommendation?" he said at last, with a barely suppressed sigh in his voice. He still had not even glanced at the one-page summary I had given him earlier in the meeting. After all, paperwork could be rewritten. First he needed to know how potentially serious the repercussions were.

"Our legal counsel has reviewed the company's liability in this matter, and is recommending Bill's termination."

"What?" he exploded. "Are you people crazy? There is no way I am going to fire Bill. Isn't going to happen. Period. So what else have you got?"

Over the next few days, there was a lot of back and forth between the CEO, our attorneys and me, and finally, an excruciatingly awkward meeting between the CEO and Bill G. and myself. Marvin wanted to hear, from Bill's own mouth, his version of these events. He wanted me to be present partly because he wanted a third-party there to protect both himself and the company, and also because he was angry with me, and wanted me to have to endure Bill's denials in front of him.

I said some pretty urgent prayers during those days, for wisdom, patience, guidance and strength to do the right thing, even if it cost me my job. I knew that Bill and the CEO went back for years, and I was a fairly recent arrival. I was aware that the CEO would have preferred it, if HR had somehow managed to sweep this whole thing under the rug, and go along to get along.

However, I had not gotten into employee relations to go along with the status quo. I had entered that field because it turned out that I had a knack for understanding both the business model in place and the human dynamics that could make it work more smoothly. I recognized positional power, and knew that those without it were vulnerable to abuse. Someone who knew the stakes, and understood the game, had to be willing to take a stand from time to time. It turned out that sometimes that person had to be me.

During that three-way meeting, Bill was arrogant as always, unapologetic, railing on about snivelers and whiners, and demanding that I explain myself to him. Who did I think I was? A newbie causing him all this grief. He glared at me from across the conference table, where now the one-page summary document was on full display, a copy in front of each of us. Raising his voice, as I had been told he often did when anyone challenged him, he roared at me, "How do you think anyone like you can prove what kind of manager I am?"

I looked at him and I looked at the CEO and said regretfully, "I'm sorry, Bill. But I don't need to. I think you just did that." The meeting ended quickly thereafter.

The crisis reached the boiling point when, after days of stalling, the CEO called me back into his office and asked what I was doing to "resolve the issue." I responded that our legal firm of "X, X, and Y" was still recommending termination. I was still waiting for his approval to proceed.

"The last time I checked," Marvin said sarcastically, "X, X, and Y doesn't run this company. I do."

I waited quietly. I said nothing as there was really nothing more to be said. The facts were what they were and they weren't going to change.

Finally he said, "Here is what we are going to do. Bill is going to be suspended without pay for two weeks. He is going to be placed on probationary status, and if there is another substantiated complaint against him, he is out of here. That is as far as I am willing to go, and it is all that I think the facts warrant. Go write it up."

"Do you want to be present, when this disciplinary decision is presented to Bill?" I asked.

"No. We're done here."

I wrote it up, legal reviewed it, I delivered it to Bill the following day, and he went home for two weeks. I wish I could say he came back a changed man, but this is the real world. He came back resentful, angry and full of wrath. But he did not retaliate against any of his staff. I checked in regularly to assure that was not occurring. Six months later he abruptly took early retirement.

The CEO, Marvin, and I had taken one another's measure and, while not exactly happy about what we had learned of one other, there was a cautious respect. I worked there another decade. And there came a time when he would call me, when things had gotten out of hand, and he had gotten wind of it, and he would simply say, "Marsha, go look into this and tell me what you find."

Sometimes I hated my job. Sometimes I loved my job. But I was never bored with my work. It was work worth doing and doing to the very best of my ability.

Tending Tip: When the pressure is greatest that is often the best time to say the least.

> *"Why should prayer and work be looked upon as conflicting human enterprises? The truth is that we can pray while we work, and we can work while we pray."* – Elton Trueblood [11]

Chapter Ten
Dress For Success — Or Not

I know of no other organizational policy that can make a grown man or woman cry like a baby, like that of the company dress code. How I hated the very thought of it. It was inevitably a no-win proposition. More accurately, it was a guaranteed lose-lose. As the HR lady, and currently the in-house policy wonk, I was going to hate re-writing the wretched thing, and the employees were absolutely going to hate following it. On a daily basis it was going to be ignored and deliberately flouted ... somewhere by someone.

People were going to get warned, and written up, and even upon rare occasion dismissed over it. All anyone had to do to make me break out in hives was to suggest that we were going to need to revisit the dress code. Oh, please, just kill me now!

Why then – a sane person might reasonably ask – bother to have such a thing? Trust me when I tell you that there is not enough time or wisdom to ever fully answer that. Dress requirements are as ancient as religious ceremonial robes and as current as this week's article, informing us according to news reports, that the U.S. military once again updated their own lugubrious dress codes. Frankly, I have learned over decades dealing with dress codes that it is better to laugh over them than to cry over them. And I have done both. Sometimes hysterically – in private. Just saying.

Early one morning my boss, Glenda, called me into her office and frantically motioned silently for me to close the door behind me. I had not even had time to put away my purse and coat, so I could hardly imagine what could have happened this early in the workday to provoke such an extreme reaction. She was ordinarily a fairly laid-back kind of boss.

"Marsha, you've got to do something about Trudy", she stated a bit breathlessly.

I had just recently been assigned a pool of secretaries and administrative assistants to supervise, and Trudy was among them. "What has she done this early in the day?" I asked completely perplexed. It wasn't even 8:00 o'clock.

"Have you *seen* her, yet?"

"Well, no. I just got here. What's the problem?"

Glenda told me to go find Trudy and the problem would be self-evident. I thought that generally enough trouble managed to find my desk uninvited; so why would I go looking for it? Nevertheless, I went in search of the day's first challenge.

Trudy was an experienced administrative assistant. Her husband was a highly successful businessman, and Trudy made it plain to all who would listen that she did not "have to work", but only did so because she wanted to get out of the house and so that she could support her extensive shopping habits without dipping into the household budget. Despite her somewhat arrogant air she was, nevertheless, an excellent admin assistant and she knew it.

I put away my personal items and headed for the break room where the first-cup-of-the-day coffee rituals were being enacted. I found my cup and started toward the coffee maker when I was stopped dead in my tracks.

There was Trudy, sipping daintily, wearing a get up that could only be described as macabre – at least for an office setting. She was clothed in black from head to toe, black leather. Clothed might not quite convey the picture, as she appeared to have been poured into her garments while standing. I had no idea how she planned to sit down. Perhaps they weren't real, perhaps they had been spray painted on. A black leather, thigh-high, skirt and matching jacket were atop black snakeskin stiletto heels. The heels were fetchingly paired with black fishnet stockings. Fishnet? I could not recall ever having seen such a thing in an office. Or anywhere else other than on TV. I groaned inwardly, thinking it was only Monday. It was going to be a long week.

I poured my coffee first, as I figured I was going to need all the help I could get, and then asked Trudy if she could stop by my office when she had finished her coffee. I took my cup back to my office to await her arrival. A few minutes later she appeared at my desk and I had no more idea of what to say to her than I had when I had first seen her ensemble. All she needed was a whip and a chair and she was ready to play dominatrix with the best, or the worst, of them, I thought glumly.

"Ah, Trudy, I must say that is a very interesting outfit you are wearing today. Fairly unique, actually."

"Yes," she preened. "Isn't it?"

"We do have a bit of a problem, though. It just isn't what you would call office wear. I don't want to offend you, or embarrass you, but it just won't work here."

Trudy bristled and said, "I don't know what you mean. Do you have any idea what this outfit cost? This is real leather! I paid over a thousand dollars at Nordy's for this suit alone." So familiar was she with the upscale department store in the mall, located directly across the street from our offices, she referred to Nordstrom's by a nickname. I really didn't want to think about what the stilettos and the fishnets had set her back.

"This isn't about whether your outfit is expensive, it is about whether or not it is appropriate for an office setting. I've been asked to let you know that our VP doesn't think it is."

Trudy had only been with us for about a month, and had apparently only now become comfortable enough to allow her real tastes to emerge. She proceeded to inform me that she had begun to suspect that this office was really old-fashioned about a lot of things. She mentioned that someone had made a snarky remark to her, just last Friday, because she was a few minutes late getting to her desk. A co-worker, watching from an office window, had made a snide comment to Trudy about taking too long getting the canvas cover on her fire engine red Corvette, before finally entering the office.

"Then there was the fuss just because I asked why we didn't have a grinder so that we could at least drink *fresh* coffee. And now this. What do you people want from me, anyway?" By this time she was incensed at the injustice of it all.

"Trudy, I am sorry that you are upset. But I am going to have to ask you to go home and change into something more appropriate for the office."

"But," she spluttered, "That will take up nearly my entire lunch hour, driving home and back."

"No, I don't think you understand. You need to go home and change now. Not at lunch time."

She didn't know it, but Glenda, our VP, had sent me an email, while I waited for Trudy to arrive from the break room, informing me that we had corporate visitors coming today and she was *not* going to have them thinking we were running a bordello out of some back office.

Trudy and I exchanged a few more minutes of fashion repartee with the upshot being that she quit. On the spot. I expressed my regrets and calmly asked for her ID badge and accompanied her to her desk so that she could retrieve her Coach handbag. After confirming the mailing address to which I could send her final check, she stormed out casting withering glances left and right. Sometimes my job made me laugh.

Dress codes were always supposed to be about one thing: appropriate and safe workplace attire. Almost always, they turned out to be about something else entirely. Sometimes it was about a fashion statement, other times an ego trip—or is that redundant?

California, the environs where I plied my trade, generally maintained a policy prohibiting the wearing of "flip-flops" in the office. Likewise, mules, slides or any type of shoe without a strap or back of some sort. The reason was simple – safety first. Offices frequently have cords, wires, and other floor hazards scattered here and there, despite all our safety seminars. It was considered too dangerous to compound the problem by schlepping around in flip-flops. Plus, they just did not convey a professional image. However, during our scorching summers, inevitably a few employees would attempt to slip by the dress code and wear them to work. Given that the most frequently worn shoes for women in offices at that time were three-inch heels, there were days when I did not blame them for trying. But the rules existed for a reason.

One long-time employee, Darlene, decided rules/schmules and sneaked in wearing her favorite flip-flops. This was not difficult to do, since she was spending most of her days in a basement storage area cataloguing inventory. She rarely saw anyone outside her work team down there, and none of them seemed to object, so she figured she could safely ignore the rule.

Sure enough, on about the third or fourth day of her seemingly modest defiance, she slipped and fell over some items stacked in plain view, but which had somehow escaped her notice. The post-accident investigation clearly established that there were brightly colored safety strips throughout the area, to caution folks to watch their step. The area was well-lighted and clear of any debris. This plus the fact that she had already been working in that same area for several days prior to the accident, and thus was familiar with the layout, meant that it was a simple accident. Darlene misstepped, lost her balance and fell, while wearing her flip-flops. She had also, unfortunately, broken her left leg.

Darlene promptly sued the company for workplace negligence, pain and suffering, inadequate supervision, and everything else her attorney could think of to throw into the mix to the tune of a demand for a million dollars. I spent the next two and a half years in discussions, depositions, and finally a settlement hearing. She basically wanted the company to pay her for the rest of her life, while she did nothing except bemoan her misfortune.

We objected to that proposition and eventually she walked away (with a somewhat dramatic limp that seemed to come and go as needed for effect) with nothing more than medical expenses covered – for life – for anything related to the broken leg.

All over a pair of flip-flops. Suffice it to say – I hate flip-flops to this day. Do not own a pair and never will.

Tending People

I had first become apprised of the criticality of an appropriate dress code very early in my career, while managing a local dental practice. There were two dentists, three chairside assistants, two part-time dental hygienists, and a high school student who served as an after-school office assistant. As the office manager, I completed the employee roster.

After I had been there some months, the part-time high school girl graduated and then quit as she prepared to leave for college. I was tasked with finding her replacement, preferably someone who could stay more than one year and who showed some aptitude for the duties required. It was to be my first hire. After interviewing several candidates, one seemed more eager than the rest to obtain the position, despite the fact that I had described it in no-nonsense terms: routine filing, putting away supplies, and even scrubbing down the operatories (treatment rooms) at the end of each day. She averred that she was ready and willing to do whatever was needed.

Mirandeena was seventeen years old and told me that she really needed the job because she and her single-parent father had just recently moved to our little town. She didn't yet know anyone, and furthermore, she could really use the money for "school supplies and such" because her dad had only been able to obtain part-time employment and things were a little tight at home.

My heart was touched and I hired her, more or less, on the spot. Events later proved that my well-meaning compassion was to be completely eclipsed by my culpability in making a poor selection. But it was my very first hire and I did not have a clue.

The next afternoon Deena, as she preferred to be called, arrived for work, or at least I was fairly sure it was Deena. However, she looked nothing like the demure young lass I had interviewed just the day before. *That* girl had worn a simple skirt and a white blouse, set off by nicely styled hair and very little makeup.

The young woman who presented at my desk the following afternoon nearly startled me off my swivel chair. It took a moment to locate her eyes, as they were obscured with mascara, eye shadow and liner that had evidently been applied with a trowel, and those eyes were hidden behind wildly teased hair falling in every direction from an elaborate up-do, with copious bangs which nearly reached her chin. And her fingernails had somehow miraculously grown an inch overnight and were painted a bright purple!

How was she going to see to do the filing? How could she scrub sinks with those nails?

As my gaze slipped below her chin, I was even more startled to observe ample cleavage on open display, with her blouse cinched in tightly with a belt that sported various shaped silver studs. The belt was atop a skirt that extended about … well that was another issue, it didn't extended nearly far enough, but rather ended abruptly somewhere around mid-thigh. Or above. I really did not allow my glance to linger as I tried to decide how to address the situation.

Before I could do more than say hello, and remind her that cleaning was part of her duties, she smartly whipped out an apron she had brought with her and proceeded to tie it around her waist. I quickly turned around as though to pick up a file folder, so that she could not see me struggling to hide a chuckle at the apron she had just donned. It belonged in a French farce rather than a dental office. It was a sheer little number, surrounded by ruffles and she was clearly pleased with her accoutrement. I didn't know what to say, so I said nothing.

For two more days she appeared each afternoon, flitted about the establishment hither and thither, seemingly very busy but accomplishing little. That would have been a problem in and of itself; but it was not the worst of it. Her outfits had gotten more risqué each day. Each spandex mini-skirt was more miniscule than its predecessor, and by that third day it was more like a very wide belt than a skirt.

On that third afternoon of her employment, just before time to close the office, the managing doctor called me into his private office near the back of the building.

"Marsha, this just isn't working out. Deena will have to go."

"But she has only been here three days," I protested. "Maybe she will get better with a little more training, if we just show some patience."

"No," he said firmly. "I don't think so."

"Surely you aren't going to just fire her?"

"No, I am not. You hired her and it is up to you to fire her."

I was horrified. It had never crossed my mind that if I made a poor hiring decision, I would also have to be the one to undo it. Why hadn't someone told me this?

"Oh, please. Can't we just give her a couple of weeks or so, to see if she can learn to adapt?"

"Marsha, here is the thing. I work all day long, with a high-speed drill, about three inches from the patient's brain. It is entirely possible that if she comes sashaying past the treatment room door in one of those tiny spandex mini-skirts she seems so fond of, and if I happen to glance up just at that moment, well … someone could end up with a pre-frontal lobotomy." He managed to say this with only the hint of a slight grin.

"You are serious. I have to fire her?"

"Yes. And it would be better to do it sooner rather than later. There is no point in letting her think she is settling in."

"You mean do it today?"

"Yes. As soon as the last patient has gone, please let her know that we will not be needing her again. Period."

Thus, at about five fifteen that afternoon, Deena and I were the last two in the office. I was posting the fees received for the day and she was giving a fine impression of actually doing some filing.

"Deena, we need to talk."

"Sure, what about?"

"Well, I am afraid I have something difficult to tell you. Your employment here just isn't working out."

"What do you mean?" she asked all wide-eyed and innocent. Apparently it had not occurred to her that she was not succeeding.

"Well, to be honest with you, your style of dress is just not acceptable for a professional office. It has caused some complaint among the rest of the staff, and ... well ... you just don't seem to be well-suited to this type of work. I am sorry to have to tell you this, but the doctor made a decision earlier today," (I decided I might as well throw him under the bus since he had already left the building) "and he has asked me to let you know that we will not be needing you any longer."

Bug-eyed she shrieked at me, "What do you mean 'you won't be needing me'? Do you mean I am fired?"

"I wouldn't put it quite like that, but yes, we have to let you go. Today is your last day."

With this she whirled around, wildly grabbing her purse, and as she stomped out the door she cried "But I bought an apron."

Thus began my career-long aversion to the dreaded dress codes and the complications created by them never seemed to diminish in the following years. Not infrequently they became substantially worse, truth be told. Still many years later, I would smile to myself (when current dress-code challenges again came my way) at the memory of the phrase, "… but I bought an apron." Indeed, she did.

Suffice it to say, I truly hated dress codes. Over time I became well experienced in tending to employees over foolishness, incompetence, anxiety, arrogance, negligence, dishonesty, theft or what have you. But I never became comfortable telling another person, male or female, how they should dress for work.

Tending Tip: If, unfortunately, it falls to you to advise another about how to dress on the job, you may want to keep in mind the following– this is about the company's professional standards, not a personal preference on your part. If there are safety issues involved, emphasize those over any nit-picking about details. (You can always laugh, or cry, later – privately.)

"… *Clothe yourselves with compassion, kindness, humility, gentleness and patience."-* Colossians 3:12. Best wardrobe choices ever. Sometimes harder to wear than a hair shirt.

Chapter Eleven

CARING NOT CODDLING

It is a self-evident fact, or at least one might think it should be, that when a person is being paid for an agreed upon number of hours per day or week, the time for which the employee is paid belongs to the employer. Obviously this refers only to an hourly not a salaried employee, the latter being paid to produce an agreed upon amount of work, or to perform supervisory or management responsibilities, regardless of the amount of time involved.

Thus, it never failed to surprise me every time an hourly employee used paid company time for personal pursuits and then, upon-being taken to task for it, acted affronted that we should even inquire. I am not talking about the too frequent personal phone calls or playing video games that routinely took place. That annoyed me but it didn't surprise me. No, I refer to those individuals who simply leave the work place to go off and do whatever during work hours, without permission or reporting it after the fact, and then turn in their time card as though they have been hard at work the whole time. It is variously known as gold-bricking, taking a lo-o-o-ng lunch break or, to put it more bluntly, falsifying a time card. It costs employers hundreds of millions each year.

Yet some employees seem to think it has nothing to do with them whatsoever, all evidence to the contrary.

One such employee, Sondra, was recovering from a workplace injury, and was scheduled for physical therapy (P/T) sessions three times per week during working hours. We did all we could to arrange her schedule to accommodate these appointments. She had sustained a fairly straightforward "slip and fall" on-the-job injury and the original doctor's note had indicated that three to four months of physical therapy (P/T) treatments should take care of the problem. Various work activities were assigned to other team members so that Sondra did not have to stoop, bend, or reach above the shoulders; nor could she be expected to sit for periods of time beyond thirty minutes without a stretch break, per the doctor's instructions. All this from a relatively minor mishap.

However, we were now nearing the one-year mark since Sondra's accident, with no end in sight for the ongoing P/T appointments accompanied by the other accommodations. The supervisor, Yvette, was still sending in the required doctor's notes to the HR office and Workers Compensation Benefits (work comp) continued to pay for all approved treatments. Still, we could see no real improvement and Yvette began to pay closer attention to these three-times-per-week absences.

Nonetheless, it was not company vigilance that ended Sondra's lengthy recovery. Rather it was a fellow employee, Kendra, who ran into Sondra shopping in K-Mart at 2:00 in the afternoon, when she was supposedly at a medical appointment, which disrupted Sondra's leisurely recuperation. Kendra did not approach Sondra directly, as she had become increasingly difficult to work with over the past several months. Instead Kendra went to Yvette, their mutual supervisor, and reported the encounter saying that on her day off she had encountered Sondra shopping, and asked whether Sondra was also on a day off? Nooooo, it seemed Sondra was supposed to be attending one of her never-ending P/T sessions, when Kendra had spotted her at K-Mart.

Yvette called me and the wheels of justice began to grind, albeit not as quickly as one might have hoped. First we had to confirm whether Sondra did, in fact, have a scheduled appointment upon that day. Perhaps there had been a mix-up or a last minute change of schedule. The doctor could not speak to us about her treatment due to HIPAA (Health Insurance Portability and Accountability Act of 1996) regulations. We were only the employer. But he could and would speak with a work comp representative since work comp was the authorizing (paying) party.

Calls were made, schedules were checked and re-checked, and three days later we were in possession of documents attesting that there had been no appointment upon the day in question. We were further informed that Sondra's P/T treatments had been reduced some three months earlier, and her appointments had finally ended altogether nearly six weeks ago.

Next, we contacted the timekeeper in payroll, who was tasked with maintaining the files on all work comp covered doctor appointments, and requested that she forward the file on Sondra to my attention in the HR office. Yvette and I sat down and examined the notes, beginning with those nearly a year old, then comparing them with those of recent months. Clearly some copying and fudging had occurred.

Still, an employer must not do or say anything to an employee with a work-related injury that may be construed as retaliation against the employee for having reported an injury and/or for missing time from work for legitimate treatment. Nor should they. But this was blatant fraud. However much we were tempted to rush into scalding denouncement mode, caution was called for.

Instead, we allowed Sondra to leave for two more fictitious appointments that same week, and then on Friday afternoon we requested her attendance in the HR conference room. The CEO himself once told me that the last place on earth he ever wanted to be was in the HR offices at 4:00 o'clock on a Friday afternoon. "Nothing good ever happens in one of those meetings," he sagely opined. Too often true.

As the three of us sat down that afternoon, Sondra looked mildly put out at having to attend the meeting, when everyone knew her flex schedule allowed her to leave around 4:00 p.m. What was this about, anyway? Clearly, she was another of those from the school of thought that the best defense is a good offense. First, we inquired about her progress in recovering from her accident.

"Oh, it has been a lot harder than I thought it would be. I'm still not feeling that great some of the time," Sondra dryly responded.

"Sondra," I said in a measured tone, "it has come to our attention that your treatment seems to be taking a good deal longer than originally anticipated. Has there been some problem that we don't know about?" Now she became suspicious and her eyes narrowed as she replied, "You would have to ask my doctor about my progress. All I know is that it still hurts a lot."

"And are you still seeing your physical therapist regularly?"

Sondra tersely replied, "Of course I am. Don't you people keep records?"

"Actually, yes, we do. And in reviewing those records we noticed that you are still reporting three two-hour sessions each week. Is that correct," I inquired?

"Yes, I guess so. Why?"

"Well, as I said, we have some questions. For instance, last Monday were you at a P/T appointment?" I queried as benignly as I could manage.

"I guess so. I would have to check my calendar."

"And what time was the appointment?"

"Oh, I don't remember exactly," Sondra offered vaguely. "I think from one to three or something like that."

"And it is our understanding that your appointments are only for one hour, but the company allows you an additional half-hour each way to drive to and from those appointments. So you have an approved two-hour window to be absent from work, for your P/T sessions. Is that correct?"

By now she was looking a little sullen. "I guess so."

"Then, Sondra, can you explain why it would be that you were seen shopping at around two o'clock that afternoon in the middle of a one to three o'clock P/T absence?" Clearly we were now getting to the nitty-gritty of the situation, so I tried to keep any accusatory tone from seeping into my question. Just asking for clarifying information, thank you. Long experience had taught me that the more outrageous the behavior in question seemed to be, the more matter-of-fact and calmly that behavior should be broached.

"What do you mean? Seen shopping? I mean, I may have stopped at a store for a couple of minutes to pick up something. I really don't see where that is any of your business."

"We are asking because you reported on your time card that you were at a doctor's appointment, but you were seen shopping during the time you were supposed to be at a medical appointment. That is a problem for you."

Stiffening with indignation Sondra said "I really don't see what the big deal is. Why are you harassing me? I got hurt on the job and I have a right to go to my medical treatments. Besides which it is almost the holidays, so I stopped off to do a little Christmas shopping. It is none of your business when and where I do my holiday shopping and I don't appreciate you giving me the third-degree."

"Sondra, you are correct in that it would be none of my business at all," I said, "when and where you do your Christmas shopping, as long as you were doing it on your own time. But wasn't this on company time? Time for which you were being paid to work?"

"Oh, for crying out loud. Are you going to tell me that I am being written up for stopping for five minutes on my way back to work? That's pretty (expletive) if you ask me." Sondra evidently felt we were pouring salt on her wound, as it were, so she indulged in some fairly salty language.

Now her supervisor, Yvette, spoke up. "Sondra, this is not about five minutes. We have documentation showing that your physical therapy appointments were reduced in frequency about three months ago, first from three times a week to twice a week, and then to only once a week. Six weeks ago they were completely discontinued. I have reviewed your time cards for the past three months, and you have been taking off work three times a week, for two hours each time, when in fact most of those times you did not have a medical appointment. That is called falsifying a time card."

"What?" Sondra shouted at us. "Are you telling me you are picking through my time cards now, just to punish me for getting hurt on the job?" Clearly, she knew where the tension points in the employer-employee relationship were and just which buttons to push.

"No." Yvette replied, "We are not punishing you for getting hurt, nor for seeking treatment for your injury. But we are holding you accountable for turning in dishonest time cards for the past eleven weeks. The employee handbook makes it very clear that turning in a false time card is a terminable offense." I truly appreciated working with a supervisor who demonstrated self-control in a trying situation, but who also knew how and when to draw the line.

Sondra looked nearly apoplectic at this point. No show of embarrassment, much less remorse, for getting caught. No guilty glances for cheating. Just sheer outrage that we would hold her to account. I reviewed her rights with her, gave her the information required by law, and handed her a final paycheck.

As she left the conference room, I could not help but notice her limp seemed vastly improved from when she had walked in some twenty minutes earlier. Sometimes my job made me sigh.

This outcome was in stark contrast to a call I received from a seasoned and effective manager, Doug Ray, who worked at one of our more remote locations. He ran a skilled team of mechanics who maintained a lot of specialized heavy equipment. They were housed in an industrial complex some miles from our main corporate campus. He called to ask if I would drive out to their location to assist him in dealing with a young female employee. I knew this guy and knew he would not call without good reason.

When I arrived at his office, a small cluttered work space in the corner of a huge barn-like warehouse, Doug Ray seemed to be alone. It turned out that he was. After glancing around and not seeing anything on fire or anyone in tears, I smiled and asked, "What's happening, Doug Ray?"

"I think I am going to need some help in letting Jennifer go."

Again, looking around and not seeing anyone, I asked "Where is she by the way?"

"That is just the problem. I don't know." Doug Ray offered this stoically without fanfare.

"You mean she just walked off the job without any notice? Has she quit?"

"No, I don't think so," he replied. "You see, we have a fairly unique set up out here at Building D. Most members of my crew are out in the field, repairing machinery at the site, or arranging to tow it back here to the garage. I come in early in the morning, review assignments with them, and then spend most of my day out in the field doing eyes-on supervision, rotating among the teams. Some of this stuff we work on, a single piece of it costs a half a million to replace, so I am pretty involved in overseeing repairs. That means that for much of the day, Jennifer is here alone answering phones, entering time cards into payroll, processing warranty claims, etc. Until recently, any time I called in she usually answered the phone and could locate the information I needed pretty quickly."

"And now?" I asked.

"Well, about a month ago, I called her and she didn't respond. She did call me back about an hour later with the information I had asked for on a voice mail I left her. I didn't think much of it. But then a couple of weeks ago, it happened again. I called in for some data, she didn't answer and it went to voice mail. I left a detailed message explaining what I needed, but by the time I got back here to the yard it was after 5:00 and Jennifer had gone home. She left the data I requested on my desk. But she didn't leave any explanation as to where she had been when I called. There was a third incident last week.

Now today, I called here about 2:00 and when I didn't get her, I decided to drive back here. She was nowhere to be found, and she did not leave a note saying where she was or when she would be back. I now realize that this may have been going on for some time, but I was too busy to notice. I just didn't give it much thought, especially in light of the fact she does do a good job maintaining our warranty records, processing parts orders, etc."

I thought a moment and said, "So you think she is doing her work, and then on the chance that maybe you won't call, she is just taking off early?"

Doug Ray said thoughtfully, "Well either that, or she's just leaving for an hour or two and then coming back and not saying anything about it, figuring I won't notice because I am gone so much." We both knew where this might be going, so I just asked, "Have you looked at her time cards over the past month?" He said he had and they showed no partial-day absences. We looked at the clock and it was now about 4:00 p.m. Jennifer had been absent for at least two hours without notifying her supervisor.

Doug Ray said he would be here until at least 5:00–would I mind staying in case she came back? I agreed, but at almost 5:30 we looked at each other, shaking our heads, and went home. We had agreed that the next day at 10:00 a.m. I would return, and he would meet with me and Jennifer. The next day, as soon as we sat down with her, she began to tremble, saying "I'm in big trouble, aren't I?"

"Well, Jennifer," I began, "we do have some serious questions to ask you. First, where were you yesterday afternoon between say 2:00 and 5:00 p.m.?"

She began to cry. "I went home for a while. Then I decided I would do some grocery shopping. Since I live nearby I swung by here and nothing seemed to be going on, so I went on home for the day. I know it was wrong. I was supposed to be here to answer the phones, but it was dead so I thought it wouldn't really matter."

Now Doug Ray began to weigh in. "Where were you on October 3rd from 1:00 to 3:00 p.m.? I know you returned because although I could not reach you around 1:30, when I got back later you were here."

Jennifer tearfully told us that over the past few weeks, since she was often alone here all day, she had begun to leave – at first for just an hour, then for longer periods of time, until yesterday, when she left at 1:30 right after finishing her paperwork. She thought Doug Ray would think he had just missed her when he got back to the office around 5:00 or a little after.

I felt sorry for this young woman, but not so sorry that we were willing to overlook repeated dishonesty. Doug Ray had already made up his mind. Despite television shows where someone seems to take great satisfaction, even glee, in saying "You're fired" – I don't believe I have ever said those words to anyone. Yes, I have had to dismiss, for cause, a number of people over the years. But I never enjoyed it, did not take any satisfaction in it. In management training sessions, I often taught our managers that termination was the workplace equivalent of capital punishment. There is no more appeal and almost no way to undo the damage, or make it right, if we get it wrong. We were depriving that individual of the ability to earn a living at our company. When I had to let someone go, I always kept in mind that the manner in which it was done could affect them for a long time.

"Jennifer, we are very sorry that it has to be this way, but I think you know that you are going to lose your job here." She shook her head "yes".

"You have made a series of choices over the past few weeks, and those choices involved falsifying your time cards, reporting time worked when you were not here. Isn't that correct?"

She again nodded.

"I am so sorry," she said. "And I am ashamed of myself. I don't know why I thought this would be okay."

"It is very early in your career, Jennifer, and you have made a serious mistake. I know that this meeting is awful for you to go through, but here is the thing. If you will learn from this mistake, you will never have to go through another meeting like this one for the rest of your life. You will not have to admit to lying to your employer, or to taking advantage of your boss. You can move past this and do a good job wherever you go next. Do you understand?"

She was so young and inexperienced she did not even ask about what we might tell a prospective employer who might call us. So I went over the process for filing an unemployment claim, handing her the EDD (Employment Development Department) brochure as I did so, and I also told her that if her next employer happened to call us for a job reference, we would be very circumspect in what we told them. Then I asked her a question that really surprised her. "Jennifer, if we do receive such a call, what do *you* think we should tell them?"

She had her head down, staring at her lap, but she had stopped crying. Now she took in a breath and looked up to meet my eyes. "I think maybe you could tell them that I do good work. I am fast and accurate. That I made some mistakes that cost me my job, but that you think maybe I have learned from them and could be a good employee."

I looked at Doug Ray and he nodded affirmatively.

"Usually, when someone has been let go for cause" I replied, "that is for breaking the rules or doing something wrong, we just say 'no comment', when we get a reference call in the HR office. Generally we will confirm dates of employment and job title, nothing more. But with your permission, I will let my staff know that any reference call about you is to come directly to me, and I will tell a prospective employer exactly what you just said. No more and no less. Is that fair?"

Jennifer said that she thought it was more than fair and left.

We all do the wrong thing sometimes. We don't just make inadvertent mistakes, but we make deliberately bad choices, knowing even as we as we do it that it is wrong. We then need forgiveness and grace. Most people, unlike Sondra, who lose their job for lying, cheating, or stealing, already know they have done something wrong. There is no need to harangue or humiliate them. When we humiliate someone, we automatically assure that they will become bitter over it – and that is a fruit that inevitably bears poisonous seeds.

However, I do believe in holding people accountable. It is the tough-love side of tending people. Caring about employees – or people in general – does not equate to coddling them. It means to treat them with respect and dignity, even when they have compromised their own integrity. When I fail, as I must from time to time, I can only hope that someone will extend some grace to me. Again, as Max DePree wrote, "*Covenantal relationships tolerate risk and forgive errors.*"

Tending Tip:
- Forgiveness in the workplace does not mean there are no consequences for wrong-doing. But it does mean that accountability can be administered without mean-spirited humiliation.

- *"We all stumble in many ways."*–James 4:3. I have barked my shins on my own stupidity and misdeeds more than once. The bruises lingered, but I learned from them.

Chapter Twelve
A Rotten Attitude Stinks

Accountability is a universal expectation on any job. One must be willing to answer for one's words and actions. Too often accountability seems to only go one way, downward from managers to supervisors to line employees. But accountability must go both ways, in order for the organization to function effectively. Those in charge of managing the projects and goals of the organization need to take responsibility for the manner in which they achieve those outcomes, by the way in which they lead or mentor others.

One hoped that there would be an ongoing dialogue and clearly communicated expectations between the supervisor and the one being supervised. Unfortunately, I often hoped in vain. To suddenly spring some kind of corrective action upon an employee who has never been made aware that his/her performance is lacking is unfair. Unfortunately, it is also all too common. A supervisor would, ideally, first speak with an employee and advise him/her using specific examples of the ways in which he/she is not performing to standards. Only after a genuine attempt has been made to bring any short-comings to the employee's attention, should further corrective action be considered.

A Rotten Attitude Stinks

So I was once again somewhat dismayed, each time I came across a long-time supervisor or manager (sometimes with the company for ten or even twenty years) who had never held an employee accountable for poor performance. Often in these situations, it would emerge that when dealing with a problem employee, the supervisor either ignored the issue, transferred them to another unsuspecting department, or "rode their tails" until the offender quit. Psychologists might label this passive-aggressive behavior. Regardless of the label used to describe it, it amounted to supervisory negligence. When a supervisor or manager presented a problem of that nature to me, asking me to step in and "take care of it," I would instead engage them in a dialogue that would begin something like the following.

1. "Can you tell me how long this employee has been displaying this behavior?"
2. "What actions have you already tried to get him to correct the problem?"
3. "What it would look like to you, if this employee was able to turn his performance around and succeed in your department?"

Their answers usually went something like:

1. "Oh, I don't know, months? Years? Since they were hired?"
2. "Well, I told him once to knock it off."
3. "Huh?"

Holding managers and supervisors accountable was always more difficult than dealing with individual employees. It often turned out that supervisors, who were subject matter experts in their specific area, had been promoted to management on the basis of their technical superiority with little or no training or experience in actually dealing with employees. This set of circumstances understandably led to significant problems for both the supervisor and the employees. One employee handbook, which shall remain anonymous, stated (in a line sometimes used as a basis for holding employees accountable): "Failure to form positive working relationships with co-workers, managers, or subordinates is considered poor performance and may result in corrective action, up to and including termination of employment." What did that actually mean? I wasn't always sure, but I was expected to make it work.

Admittedly, it is difficult to form an effective work relationship with an employee who has a bad attitude. I sometimes told supervisors that it was like being in a room with a bad odor. You could not see it, but you definitely knew it was there and so did everyone else. Take the example of Murphy, a supervisor, and Kyle, his subordinate. Upon hearing the "rotten attitude" statement, from Murphy I replied, "Okay, let's start there. Tell me what Kyle's rotten attitude looks or sounds like."

Again, with the "Huh?"

Then we would start at the beginning. "When did you first notice Kyle's bad attitude"? Murphy responded that it had been several months, maybe a year. I then asked Murphy to describe the specific incident that brought the attitude to his attention.

"I guess it was several months ago, when I assigned each team member a particular portion of a major project with a deadline for two weeks out. After I finished telling them about the assignment, I asked if anyone had any questions. One or two asked about resources they might need and about whether they could ask for some help from a member of another department. Kyle didn't ask anything, which was fine, but he sat in the back row slumped down in his chair and looked like he couldn't wait to get out of there.

Two weeks later, a few team members brought their part of the project in to me a little early, and most delivered theirs on the day it was due. But Kyle didn't turn his part in, so the afternoon of the due date, I found him and asked him about it. He said he was close but wasn't quite finished. I gave him one more day to complete it and he did. But when he turned it in he kind of flicked it (the report) onto my desk and walked away before I could ask him what had caused the delay. He was the only one who missed the deadline."

"So would you describe his behavior as resentful?" I asked Murphy.

"Yeah, that would be correct. And I overheard him griping about it to a couple of his buddies the day before he turned it in. He didn't think two weeks was enough time to get the assignment done."

"And did Kyle ever come to you to tell you that he had problems with the assignment or the deadline? Or to ask you for an extension for his part of it?" I asked.

"No, he just griped to his coworkers," Murphy replied.

"All right," I said. "Then I think in that instance, we could say that Kyle's performance was lacking in two ways:

- He resented a project assignment but did not come to you to discuss it. However, you know that he resented it because of comments he made to coworkers. This negatively impacts team morale.
- He missed the deadline, but had not requested an extension, and offered no explanation about why he missed it.

Does this sound accurate and fair?" I asked Murphy. He said it did. We wrote it up, then met with Kyle and began the corrective process, which included what is commonly known as a PIP (Performance Improvement Plan.) When Kyle realized that he was going to be held accountable, but also would be given a chance to improve his performance, he quickly turned things around and effectively worked with Murphy and the team for several more years.

Incidents like the one just described might seem like very small potatoes. But if left unaddressed they sometimes spoiled the whole bag ... and much more.

Debra was a seasoned and successful director with the company when she came to my office one afternoon to discuss a recent hire, Lance, who was a manager in the finance department. She was hearing stray comments about how difficult he was to work with and she was concerned about it. He always seemed pleasant enough whenever she interacted with him, and she had ignored it the first couple of times she caught these passing comments. But she had now heard enough rumblings that she was beginning to be concerned. Was he one of those people who really knew how to "manage upward" but was a jerk to anyone who reported to him? How about his peers, or those in other departments? She didn't know, but she wanted me to find out.

After interviewing a number of individuals within the department, including most of Lance's subordinates, a pattern emerged. (I had also interviewed several people in the department who did not report to Lance, but did report upward to Debra, so that it would not be obvious to others that Lance was being looked at.) It turned out that Lance was, indeed, effective at upward management and even maintained a half-way decent demeanor around his peers in other departments. But he was consistently disdainful or downright rude to his subordinates. He didn't ask, he told. He didn't require, he demanded. What was even more concerning than his poor supervisory skills was the fact that one or two of his team members suspected that Lance wasn't always on the up and up; in other words they suspected he was not quite honest. They had no proof of this, just an uneasy sense that something was not right.

I wrote all this up and presented it to Debra, Lance's director. I outlined the facts. Lance had been with the company less than six months, and yet he had already alienated nearly every member of his own team. Furthermore, when I interviewed him about this, he seemed unconcerned as though it were a mundane detail about which he could not be bothered. He had more important matters to which to attend.

Secondly, he was not engaged with his team. He rarely met with them as a group and almost never met with any individual one on one, meaning he was largely unavailable. He seemed to be out of the office "in meetings" quite often, but no one could say where he was during these times or who, precisely, he was supposedly meeting with. After including some specific dates, issues, and company policies which were being ignored, if not outright violated, I regretfully recommended that Debra terminate Lance's employment. He had been with the company such a short time that it would be considered a "no harm, no foul" termination. He was an at-will employee, which simply meant that he was not under contract for a specific amount of time, and he could quit or we could end his employment at any time.

Understandably, Debra expressed her disappointment and concern. She also stated that Lance had a valuable skill set, one that wasn't easily replaced and, in fact, she had had a tough time landing him in the first place. She decided that she would counsel him about his performance deficiencies and let him know that he was skating on thin ice. However, she did not believe his issues warranted termination, so she kept him on. I put a copy of the report I had given to Debra, including the memo recommending his termination, into Lance's file and that seemed to be the end of it.

Not quite two years later, Debra faced the worst crisis of her own long career, and it was precipitated by Lance's dishonesty. He had used his signing authority and position within the finance department to embezzle a large sum of money (several million dollars) and it had happened on Debra's "watch". Though she immediately fired Lance, and notified the police and senior management, the damage was done. Debra wasn't fired because she had no knowledge of the theft until it was exposed, she had derived no benefit from it, and she had been with the company for more than twenty years. She was a good employee, who had made valuable contributions for many years, but she had trusted the wrong person.

This combination of circumstances saved her job, but the scandal marred her career/reputation and she worked those last few years under a shadow. The company's reputation had taken a real blow in the court of public opinion. Even though most of the money was eventually recovered, the fact that this embezzlement had gone undetected for some time undermined confidence in our security protocols.

The company acquired a new CEO not long after all this took place, and he was doing a retro-evaluation on how all this had happened and why it went undiscovered for as long as it did. As part of that analysis, he called me one day asking about my handling of the initial complaints about Lance. He had read, he told me, the investigation report about the complaints regarding Lance, which I had done almost two years earlier. I explained our process, why I had been so concerned about his lack of appropriate managerial skills, and why I had thus recommended his termination back then.

He shocked me by telling me that there was no documentation in Lance's file to indicate that I had ever recommended his termination. The complaint report was there, but the memo was not. Someone had removed it without my knowledge. Fortunately, I had kept a back-up digital copy, which I sent to him via email while we were still on the phone. But did it really matter now? Only in so far as it bolstered my own credibility. But the damage to the company was already done.

Tending Tip: Problems of a serious nature, even seemingly small ones, don't usually just disappear. They grow, like mushrooms, in the dark places within the organization. Failure to address a small problem can lead to the development of much bigger ones; and discovery may only occur after significant damage has been done.

We are advised that *"... it is the little foxes that ruin the vineyards."* –Song of Songs 2:15.

Chapter Thirteen
Dazed And Confused

I was just coming down the hallway to my office, after conducting an 8:00 – 10:00 a.m. training class, and I was looking forward to a break. It had been a good class full of engaged employees, who honestly wanted to do the best work they could. In my view, a trainer could not ask for a better scenario. So it was a good kind of tired, the kind of satisfaction in your bones that was more important than the ache in them. I had scarcely sat down, however, when my assistant, Jill, put her head into my office and said, "You have an urgent call on line two. I would have told them you were not available until about 10:30, but they said it is really urgent – there's a crisis of some sort down at the Rancho office."

She might have delayed putting the caller through to me, not because I made a habit of dodging employees' calls, but because she knew from working with me for several years that after teaching for a couple of hours, I usually needed a few minutes to clear my head and have a cup of coffee. I thanked Jill for the heads up and picked up the phone. The voice on the other end belonged to Sean, a first line supervisor at one of our smaller retail operations, located about twenty-five miles south of where I was sitting. He was speaking in a low, tense manner, and I got the impression he was concerned about being overheard.

"Marsha, we have a situation down here and I don't know what to do about it." Sean was in his late twenties and had only been a supervisor for about a year. These small retail operations usually were staffed by twenty-somethings who were bright, eager, young go-getters with a knack for making sales. His store employed about ten or twelve people. He said he was calling about an employee named Galen.

"Okay, Sean, let's talk it through. But first I need to ask you, is anyone hurt?"

"Well, no, not exactly but someone is off the rails and it may get worse if we don't get this under control."

"I don't know who Galen is, but if he is in some kind of danger you need to hang up and call 9-1-1 right now," I immediately replied.

Sean slowed down a bit, but the tension in his voice did not let up. "I don't think we are there yet, but Galen is acting very strangely. He came in this morning all jittery and jumpy. After messing around for a few minutes he went into the back storage room. I was busy with a customer, so I didn't pay much attention to it. I figured he was checking the inventory supplies and what have you. After the customer left, I noticed that Galen had not returned to the front of the store, so I went back to see what was up. I didn't see him, so at first I thought maybe he had stepped out the back door of the shop. I checked out back and didn't see him there either.

When I came back into the storage room, I thought I heard something coming from the supply closet, some kind of whispering or something, so I went over to check it out. The door was locked, but I could hear the whispering a little louder from inside. I knocked on the door and said, 'Galen? Is that you in there?'

At first he wouldn't answer me, but just kept mumbling. I could also hear some kind of scratching noise, like he was scratching with something on the wall or the door. This was just weird, so I called to him again, 'Galen, are you okay? What's going on?' Finally, he answered and said, 'Go away. I need some time to think. Don't bother me.' And then the whispering and scratching started again. What should I do? I have a key to that door and I did try to unlock it, but as soon as I did, Galen re-locked it from the inside and again told me to go away. He has been in there for almost an hour and he won't talk to us and he won't come out. Should we just wait him out? One of the other guys suggested we had better call HR and get some advice on how to handle this."

As I considered how to respond to this situation, I could not help but think that anyone who thought that all HR nerds did was sit around and think up more rules and regulations for everyone else to follow, had never spent a single day on the real job. "Okay, Sean. Let me ask you this, is there anything in that supply closet that Galen might be able to use to hurt himself? Tools, sharp objects? Anything like that?"

"No, I don't think so. Mostly there are some old products that have been returned and a bunch of office supplies, copier toner, paper towels, stuff like that. But not much else, because the cleaning service comes in each evening and does the regular store cleaning. I guess it is possible that there might be something in there, but off the top of my head I can't really picture anything."

"Okay," I responded, "That's good. Let me think a minute."

Before I could do that, Sean asked me, "Do you think you should come down here? Maybe try to talk him into coming out? I mean I am in way over my head on this one." I thought to myself, "Who isn't?"

"Sean, I could certainly do that, but here is the thing. It is crosstown traffic all the way between my office and your store. There is just no quick way to get there and it would take me at least forty-five minutes to an hour to arrive. Anything could happen in the meantime and I would be in the car and not be able to be of any help at all. So I think maybe we just hold steady here for a minute and try to figure out what to do."

Meanwhile, I motioned to Jill to come into my office from her own (we had a large glass interior window between our two offices for just such short-hand communication when necessary) and I handed her a note instructing her to go pull Galen's file for me, and to get me the name and phone number of his emergency contact. Then I turned back to the discussion with Sean about what to do next.

"Sean, I am thinking that we may need to call the paramedics. We don't know what's happening in that closet, but we do know it isn't normal. Someone with some medical expertise probably needs to be there."

"But what if he walks out and says it was all a joke? And we have already called 9-1-1, or the police, or whoever, and he gets mad because we made him look bad?" He had a point, albeit a strange one. But I had seen that kind of nonsense a time or two and it never ended well, either for the employee or for the company.

Just about that time I heard someone else, a woman, in the background shouting, "Oh, my God. What are you doing? Go put your clothes on." And I said to Sean, frantically now, "Sean, Sean, what is happening there?" But it was no use because Sean had dropped the phone hand-set and (as I learned later) was dashing across the store trying to grab Galen, who it seemed, had suddenly emerged from his hide-out, wearing nothing but his boxers. No clothes, no shoes, nothing.

Now I could hear someone, presumably Galen, shouting incoherently something about he was on fire and needed to cool off. I also learned that Sean made a real effort to try to stop Galen, but Galen eluded him and dashed out of the stored running pell-mell toward the adjacent highway. Sean then grabbed a mobile phone and called 9-1-1. A couple of minutes later, after he had taken a quick look in the supply closet, Sean remembered that I was still on the other line and he picked up with me.

"Son of a (expletive), Marsha, he has gone crazy. He is out there in the middle of the road almost naked, with traffic whizzing by on both sides, waving his arms and shouting. We have called 9-1-1 and they should be here any minute. I have a couple of the guys out there still trying to talk him into coming off to the side of the road, where he would at least be out of the path of oncoming cars. And you should see that closet he was in for the past hour. He has scribbled stuff with a colored marker all over the walls. Odd symbols and a bunch of numbers and words that don't make any sense at all. I've never seen anything like it."

We spoke for a couple of minutes deciding what to do with the store and the rest of the staff for the remainder of the day, while waiting for help to arrive. I advised him to close down the shop until after the lunch hour, and then have those who felt they could focus enough to work, to come back at one o'clock. I advised him to send the rest of them home for the day. He hung up as he heard the police arriving.

Galen had suffered a complete psychotic breakdown as a result of a drug-overdose. He was "5150'd" meaning the police had taken him into custody and after the appropriate medical personnel had examined him, he had been remanded to a psychiatric facility for a 72-hour hold. He did, indeed, pose an immediate danger to himself and possibly others.

From that short-term facility he was transferred a few days later to a longer term psychiatric hospital. We later learned he was there for over six-months. The week after this incident, we regretfully processed his termination of employment paperwork, and mailed it to his emergency contact, his mother. Approximately a week after this, I received an irate call from Galen's mother. She was furious with the company in general, and with me in particular, because she had heard that I was the one who told Galen's supervisor to call 9-1-1 and likely because my name was on his termination paperwork.

"Do you have any idea what you people have done to my son and to his career?" she shouted over the phone. "Galen is a brilliant young man. He had a bright future until you decided to interfere in his life and make him a laughing stock in front of all of his friends at work. People like you should be the ones getting fired, not my son!" I tried to explain that we had only made the call because his safety was at risk and that, prior to making the 9-1-1 call, his supervisor had made several attempts to reason with Galen. She was having none of it.

"Well, miss high and mighty. I don't know who you think you are, but you do not run the world. We have considerable means at our disposal, and I plan to use as much of them as necessary to sue that rotten company and to sue you personally. I am going to *take your house*," she screamed at me. "Do you hear me? I am going to own you before this is all over. And right after they fire you, I plan to see to it that my son is re-hired. He was doing a great job and didn't deserve to be fired just because he had a medical issue."

Again, I tried to explain that we had only acted in what we believed to be Galen's best interests and in support of his safety. Since she was his next-of-kin and he was still hospitalized, I could reasonably assume that she now knew the circumstances of Galen's medical condition. So I reminded her that Galen had tested positive for several illegal drugs that were in his system while he was at work. That alone was a serious violation of company policy and warranted termination of employment.

After throwing several more personal insults at me, and again telling me that she was going to take my house, the call ended. I was not worried about losing my house, partly because I knew we had acted legally and appropriately. Additionally, I was covered by the company against personal legal action as long as I had acted within the scope of my duties and had not deliberately, or with malice, harmed anyone. I sighed and thought, "If I had a dollar for every time someone threatened to 'take my house' over this job, I could probably pay off my mortgage."

On a more serious note, I thought about this parent, who was so blind to her son's addiction and dysfunction that she blamed anyone and everyone who might be handy. There seemed to be no responsibility attributed to Galen for his actions, and indeed, none for herself as his mother. It was all "our fault". We were those ubiquitous "you people" who had made her son lose his job and had ruined his life. This was helicopter parenting taken to a whole new level. The elementary or high school parent who did not believe that Johnny had cheated on the test, or that Janie had been sneaking marijuana brownies to her classmates, became the parents of employees who could do no wrong. These young employees, with whom I dealt all too often, resented taking direction, resisted feedback, and generally managed to mess up their own career opportunities without any assistance from us. But the company was to blame when it all went wrong.

Exactly one year later (to the day) Galen arrived in the main lobby of the building where my office was located. (The reader may recall that he had worked twenty-five miles south of there and had thus taken the time and trouble to find out exactly where I worked.) He told the front desk receptionist that he was here to see Marsha and she asked if he had an appointment. He said no, but he didn't need one and demanded to see me immediately. Arlene, the receptionist, became sufficiently concerned that she pressed the silent alarm button under her counter, while continuing to speak with Galen. My office was located at the opposite end of the building from the front lobby, so for a few minutes I knew nothing of this.

Meanwhile, the alert signal had gone to building security, who immediately sent someone to check out what was happening in the front lobby. The director of plant security, a fellow named Chuck, had also been notified by his team and he called me to tell me that an employee, whom I had dismissed a year ago, was in the lobby demanding to see me. Chuck wanted me to know what was happening, and told me that he wanted me to steer clear of the lobby area until they had the situation resolved. I was more than a little concerned and said, "If he is asking for me by name, maybe I could just go out and talk to him. You know, calm him down a little. There are plenty of security guys around and he doesn't have a weapon, does he?"

"Marsha, we don't know what he has or doesn't have. I just want you to remain in your office until we get this handled. I have called the police and they should be here in a few minutes." By this time my boss, Helen, had heard about the commotion in the lobby, had spoken briefly with Chuck and then came directly to my office. It seemed she knew me better than I realized as she walked through my door saying, "Marsha, you are not going out there. And that is not a suggestion. I am telling you to stay in this office until this is taken care of." So I stayed put, feeling this whole thing was being blown out of proportion.

About three minutes later, in full view of dozens of employees who were now watching glued to the inside windows all along that side of the building, three police vehicles came screeching up to the main entrance, officers jumped out and quickly took Galen into custody. He had escalated before they arrived and was shouting and spewing invective, mainly toward me by name. Thankfully, the situation was defused without further incident, but I felt sorry for him as they led him away. He was so young and with so much wasted potential.

I continued to believe that we could have dealt with Galen without calling in half the local police force. That is until a few months later, when twenty two miles up the freeway, another building was breached at a different company by another hostile ex-employee. He had a gun and he shot and killed three people, including the HR manager, before anyone could prevent it.

Tending Tip:
- Sometimes, perhaps "discretion is the better part of valor."[2] And occasionally the person you had better be tending to is yourself. Pay attention and pay heed to the advice of others. It

---

[2] This saying paraphrases a statement made by the character of Falstaff in Shakespeare's Henry IV, Part 1, Scene 3. It roughly means "that caution is better than rash courage."[12]

is good to be strong, but it can be dangerous to be too confident in your own ability to defuse a situation. I learned my lesson.

An old adage: *You'd better check yourself, before you wreck yourself.*

Chapter Fourteen
Power In Ruby Red Slippers

Many of us have read about various kinds of power in an organization. Positional power (meaning the power resides in the position held rather than the person holding it), referential power (loosely meaning the ability to influence or inspire others), formal power (such as that bestowed with an oath of office as with law enforcement) and informal power (not associated with a title or vested authority, but simply through force of personality the ability to make things happen). Each of us has some instinct about who has it and who does not, especially when it comes to the workplace. It may be difficult to describe, but we know it when we see it.

Organizational power is often obvious. It is sometimes displayed in fancy office furniture, lots of diplomas or certifications on the walls, the ability to come in a little later from time to time, or to take off early on Friday afternoon to get in a quick nine-holes. Those are the trappings of power. The reality of it is found in the ability to get things done, and more often than not, to get them done through other people. In my own case, to once again quote Robert K. Greenleaf, "... *the peculiar power of my office enable[d] me to work at settling conflicts among them.*"[13] The "them" being the people I was tending in the workplace.

The power to command and control, or to persuade and influence, is the coin of the realm in a corporate setting. It can be fascinating to watch a skilled player wield power wisely and effectively to the benefit of the entire organization. It is a deflating and discouraging thing to watch pettiness and selfishness rule the roost. Sometimes power in the workplace appears in disguise. It may appear in the guise of a petite, pretty little woman, who looks like she wouldn't hurt a fly, and who would sooner cut you to the quick than look at you.

Heather was an attractive woman, who told me upon meeting her, that "she wore the ruby red slippers" around her office, and that no one was ever going to take them away from her. I immediately thought, "What a bizarre thing to say." She was not, of course, referring to literal footwear, but rather to Dorothy's slippers in the Wizard of Oz, wherein Dorothy could click her heels and make things happen. More particularly, in Heather's case she meant her special abilities for getting her own way even when it was contrary to company policy and her manager's wishes.

Her power, unlike her ruby slippers, was not imaginary; and her vanity and spitefulness knew no bounds. She had been with the company for more than two decades and everyone in that building was scared to death of her. She had been known to slam cabinet doors, throw staplers at co-workers, and generally create havoc anytime she felt like it. Once she even slapped a co-worker – and no one reported it. Upon learning of this incredible set of circumstances, I naively asked her manager, Phil, why he put up with it.

His reply was along the lines of, "Oh, no one messes with Heather. It just isn't worth the fall out." He quietly muttered something about life becoming a living hell if you stirred that particular witch's cauldron, and went back to the safety of his own office.

This was a situation that I could not overlook and the next time someone mentioned to me that Heather was on the war path, I called her into my office. We had a pleasant enough discussion about the need to work cooperatively with others, teamwork, etc. She was well mannered and smiled pleasantly at me as she left my office, clearly determined to completely ignore everything that had been said.

A few weeks later, Heather was once again using her ruby slippers to beat people about the head and shoulders, mercilessly from what I was hearing via the office grapevine. However, no one had made a formal complaint and it was assumed therefore, by one and all, that nothing could be done. I had had about enough of Heather's hissy-fits, and the negative impact on the productivity of her department; but given her lengthy tenure with the company a cautious approach was needed. I had learned that turn-over in that department was very high. After reading a few exit-interviews from the previous three years it was obvious why that was the case. The tension was high enough to rival Everest, and the manager, while always described as a nice guy, seemed powerless to mitigate the circumstances much less actually hold anyone accountable for bad behavior. Ultimately, as Phil had said, no one was prepared to mess with Heather.

I quietly began holding a series of confidential interviews, beginning with her manager and continuing on through several key members of her department, until I had gathered enough specifics with which to again request the pleasure of her company in my office. My first encounter with Heather had been an informal chat. This meeting was to be more structured.

The first few minutes of the meeting were a seemingly casual conversation about the company in general, its goals and competitive direction. Then I steered the discussion toward her own department, and explained that I had received reports that there was a lot of tension among the staff. It has been my experience that I can often save myself the effort of digging a hole, if I am simply patient enough to allow the trouble-maker to dig it for me. This was to be one of those times.

"Well, yes, there has been some tension around the unit lately," Heather acknowledged, "but that could easily have been avoided if they had just done what I told them to." She was an entry-level assistant, in a department consisting of three teams of seven or eight members each. Each team had its own supervisor, as well as the manager who was responsible for the whole unit. Yet Heather made this unadorned claim with no apparent self-consciousness.

"I see. And why would you be the one to be telling them?" I asked this as though I were genuinely perplexed.

Heather bristled and explained what she believed to be the facts-of-life regarding her department. Namely that her manager was spineless and incompetent, that the three supervisors were idiots, and that unless she ran herd on the whole mess nothing much got done. She finished off this recounting with a little huff of indignation that she was forced to explain such basics to me.

Whereupon, I began the task of explaining to her that, contrary to what she had just described, she did not run the department. It was not her job, she was not being paid to do this, and finally, she needed to remember that it was not a one-man-band but rather a team effort. I then further explained that this meeting was considered a formal verbal warning and would be noted in her file.

She nearly sneered at me, as she said incredulously, "You're *warning* me? Are you serious?"

She then launched into a tirade about how she ran the whole department single-handedly and "everyone knew it." She pointed out that, in her candid opinion, I needed to learn the lay of the land before having the temerity to approach a seasoned veteran such as herself. Her clear perspective was that I would not be able to find my way around the building without a map and a flashlight. She finished up with what she thought was her ace in the hole. "If this is a verbal warning, why isn't my manager here?"

She had a valid point there. When I had discussed this first step with Phil, and asked whether he would like to conduct the meeting, he made it plain that he was not anxious to rile her up, and wasn't sure how much good a verbal warning might do. He was afraid it might actually make things worse – both for him as her manager and for her co-workers.

I acknowledged that it was possible things might get worse before they got better, but added that they would never get better unless something was done. I explained that since Heather had been with the company for over twenty years, it was going to take a serious, consistent, and somewhat lengthy effort to dismiss her; but that given the things a significant number of people in his department had told me, this was the path we needed to pursue. He then suggested that, perhaps, it might go more smoothly if I met with her one-on-one for now. Thus, after gaining his approval to speak with her (and giving him an easy off ramp) and going over the specifics of her latest antics to assure that I had my facts straight, I agreed to meet with her alone. It was unusual; but then the whole situation was somewhat surreal.

I told Heather that Phil, her manager, had thought that this discussion might be less awkward, if we met just the two of us. However, I explained we could certainly call Phil in, if that was what she preferred. She archly declined to have Phil join in saying he was busy and she didn't want to bother him with something as silly as this.

"What exactly, and I do mean *exactly*, is it that I am being 'warned' (here she used air-finger quotes) about? Can you tell me that?"

So I did. In specific detail as to time, date, place, issue and outcome. During this exchange, I also assured her that I was aware that she was very good at the technical aspects of her job, and that this was not the issue. I told her that, while we recognized and appreciated her contributions throughout her long tenure, her interactions with her co-workers was a problem and that going forward she needed to become aware of the negative impact of her temper, her words, and her influence. These had to change – beginning now.

A few weeks later, Heather and Phil sat in my office. This time she had deliberately flouted Phil's instructions about a supply order. After deciding that he had miscalculated the amount of supplies needed for a large construction project, without telling him or a supervisor about it, she had nearly doubled the order. The departmental budget impact amounted to tens of thousands of dollars and it was going to skew his quarterly report. That was bad enough. The larger issue was her blatant insubordination.

She initially attempted to explain the incident as a miscommunication between Phil and Jay, one of his supervisors. She had done nothing wrong. It wasn't her fault if the two of them couldn't get their supply order straight. But Phil had kept a copy of the written estimate he had given Jay. And Jay had emailed the estimate and the required order to Heather and had given Phil a copy of that email. She then claimed Jay had given her a different order, verbally. When Jay refuted that claim, she said that she never received the email from him. We showed her a confirmation of receipt we had obtained in advance of the meeting from the IT folks.

One might have thought it was game over at that point. But Heather had been around a long time and had not survived without some pretty fancy footwork herself. She immediately began to hedge her bets by explaining directly to Phil (ignoring me completely), that she had only been trying to help him look good. "You know how long it can take that supplier to deliver a big order. And you remember that they accidentally shorted us on one last year, and it took nearly two weeks to get it straightened out and caused a delay on the construction site. I was just being proactive based upon our prior experience."

Oh, she was good alright. I watched Phil begin to flush and I understood how she had manipulated her relationship with him for years. A little further probing established that the inflated order was not at all about "helping Phil look good" but rather it was about making her own job easier. Large supply orders were complex, time consuming, and tedious. The fewer of them she had to process the better, so she had made it a practice to "double down" whenever she could get away with it. She figured a few extra pieces of equipment or materials laying around the warehouse couldn't be that big a deal. She used a kind of reverse just-in-time inventory philosophy. This time she had overstepped even her own vague boundaries.

We reviewed with her the facts and consequences of her actions:

a) She had deliberately ignored a direct instruction from her manager and a supervisor.
b) She had far exceeded her signing authority in initiating such a large purchase.
c) She had compounded the problem by not being honest with us about the matter.

We presented her with a written disciplinary action, informed her that she was being suspended for a week without pay, and finally let her know that any further serious breach of company policies could be grounds for termination.

As she read and signed the forms, I requested her access/ID badge, and told her that she needed to go home, now, and her suspension would begin the following day. I assured her that we would respect her privacy and that her co-workers would only be told that she was absent for a few days, but that no one would be told the details about her absence. What she chose to tell others was her business, but I cautioned her to think carefully about what she said going forward.

Although the next few weeks were relatively quiet in Phil's department, old habits die hard, and about three months later Heather once again flagrantly ignored a direct order. She also falsified a couple of documents to cover her tracks. But, at last, the supervisors and manager were coordinating their own efforts to watch each other's backs. Now that they were fully aware of Heather's bent approach to her work, they were documenting her behavior. Soon thereafter, on a quiet afternoon, after an anything but quiet meeting with her, we fired Heather. I handed her a final check along with her termination paper work. She handed me her office keys and ID badge.

The process had taken, from start to finish, about six months. She sputtered remarks about wrongful termination, lawyers, and lack of recognition for her contributions as I escorted her out the door. I expressed the company's regrets that this action had become necessary, but added that her behavior was well-documented and, should she wish to do so, invited her to have her attorney call me. We chose not to oppose her claim for unemployment benefits, despite the fact that she had been fired for cause, and we never heard from her again.

Why and how had this toxic situation been allowed to exist for years? It had come about because, although she was haughty and vindictive, she was also a skillful employee. The old complaint I had heard over and over again applied here in spades. Managers often seemed completely befuddled when telling me, "He is the best technician I have. And he is the worst employee in the unit to manage. I can't afford to lose his skill set. But I don't know how much longer I can put up with his attitude."

It fell to me to explain that there was no mystery about this at all. Often an employee who knew that his or her skills were superior to that of their co-workers, used the critical need to retain their talent, as an excuse to behave poorly because they knew they could get away with it.

Unlike comic strips regarding workplace dysfunction, which show some hapless person being tossed out of the office, it is fairly difficult to fire someone, particularly a long-tenured employee. Furthermore, it is easier to fire someone for incompetence, than it is to dismiss her because she is a complete pain in the neck to work with and everyone else is afraid of her. Heather met her deadlines, delivered her projects, and generally followed the rules – except when it suited her better to flout them.

Her manager had been new to his position when Heather came into the department. She was subtle about her abuse of power, and kept it hidden from him for several years. She also slowly but surely garnered support among those weaker than herself, but who enjoyed watching her intimidate others, as long as she left them alone. It was almost like they were watching a football game, wherein a player well-known for playing dirty was cheered by those sitting safely in the stands. Let's watch Heather take so-and-so down.

After her departure, to try to ensure that there would be no further misunderstandings about the kind of work environment we were trying to foster, we held a department wide meeting. We never mentioned

Heather by name. Of course, everyone present knew exactly what – and who – we were talking about. We outlined what had gone wrong within their department and what we planned to do to change things going forward. I was asked to speak to them briefly, once their manager and a couple of supervisors had spoken. Here is what I told them:

> We all need to earn a living and most of us appreciate being able to do that in a decent workplace. While we always emphasize safety around here, sometimes we forget to make it clear that respect is also necessary in order for each of us to do our best. Common courtesy never goes out of style and helping a co-worker when they are in a bind makes the whole department function more effectively.
>
> Your manager and your team leaders are not interested in playing "got-cha". They would rather catch someone doing something right. So would I. Going forward we want to make it clear that trying something a little different, even if it isn't the way it has always been done, seeing whether your idea might be workable, these are things we want to encourage and support.
>
> However, ego trips, favoritism, and pressure-cooker tactics are not going to be tolerated. While we recognize the value of years of service, a long employment history will not protect any of us from the consequences of our own actions, when by those actions we make it more difficult for others to do their own jobs effectively.

There have been some changes in your department in recent days and some of you were surprised to see them. Don't be. Those who work well with others are going to be the people who get ahead. Those who create roadblocks will be held accountable.

Life is full of risk-reward scenarios. Around here taking a thoughtful risk about a new idea or a different approach to an old problem will be rewarded. Taking a risk on trying to steal the credit for someone else's contribution or ignoring the rules will be handled professionally and respectfully. But it will be handled, not ignored. I look forward to working with each of you for a long time. Let's get back to work.

Over the next year, that department's productivity went up by better than fifteen percent and turnover went down by nearly thirty percent. One exit interview, from a woman whose resignation was due solely to her husband's transfer to another state, gave us the following feedback.

Exit Interview: *I only worked here for two years. But I can tell you that the first year and the second one were like night and day. When I first came here, H. ruled the roost and everyone knew it. You lived in constant fear that you might cross her and then suffer the results of that for days or even weeks. I personally know of two guys who transferred to another*

department to get away from her; and one of my co-workers went home in tears more than once because H. had been so mean to her.

I was about ready to quit when we heard she had been called in and repramanded [sic]. We couldn't believe it. A few months later, although we never heard exactly what had happened, she was suddenly gone. After the department had that meeting, things changed so much for the better that I was sorry when my husband learned he was being transferred. I can't tell you how much I enjoyed my second year here. Thanks for this chance to tell you and to say you may not have any idea what a difference one person can make – for better or worse – in a department's morale. But I saw it happen and it was huge!

She may not have known how to spell "reprimanded" but she clearly knew the difference between working in a place overshadowed by a petite, ruby-slippered bully, and one that was not. The day I read that exit interview, I loved my job.

Tending Tip: School-yard bullies grow up to become workplace bullies. Their tactics remain much the same: prey on those weaker or newer to the sandbox, leverage their skills to the disadvantage of others, and play dirty. If, as a people-tender, you are not willing to take them on, I encourage you to consider going into another line of work.

Chapter Fifteen
IMPORTANCE VERSUS VALUE

Halle was a newly-minted college graduate when she joined our team. She was barely twenty-three, but she showed potential and we were hopeful that she would find her niche in HR. She was assigned a cubicle and initially put to work reviewing resumes and scheduling interviews with job candidates. From time to time she was allowed to accompany her manager, Ned, when he conducted an employee relations meeting in order that she could learn by being in the room when the tough stuff was under discussion.

When she had been with us about three months, she asked to meet with me. Halle did not report to me, Ned did, so ordinarily I would not meet with her unless he was also present. But she had asked for a private meeting and, in case it was something of a personal nature, I agreed to meet with her.

After the initial pleasantries were dispensed with, Halle got around to what she wanted to ask me. It was simple really. As part of her personal career planning, she had just three basic questions she wanted to ask and, since I was her department head, she figured she would come straight to me.

"I was wondering how soon I can expect my first raise. And how long after that will I be eligible for a promotion? Also, how soon before I could expect to get a private office?"

The reader may wonder whether she actually did ask these things so bluntly. Yes, she did and I was taken aback to say the least. After telling myself not to give her a lecture about paying one's dues and learning the ropes, I said, "Halle, those are interesting questions and I am glad to hear that you are looking ahead. But isn't it a little early to be thinking in terms of raises and promotions? You have only worked here three months."

Halle just smiled and blithely said, "I'm a planner and I like to know where I am going."

"Well, that is generally a good thing, but your introductory/probationary period will not be over until you have worked here for six months."

"But I don't think I am being paid what I am worth," Halle asserted.

"Didn't you agree to the salary we offered just three months ago? I seem to recall you were glad to get the job offer."

"Yes, but I've learned a lot since then." Talk about boundless confidence.

"Well, all I can tell you is that it will be about nine more months before any pay raise is likely. Generally each employee is reviewed once a year, on or about the anniversary of their hire date, and any salary adjustment is considered at that time. Working here in HR you should be aware of this," I offered dryly.

"What about a promotion? And a private office? I really don't much like working in a cubicle and I would enjoy having my own office. After all, Ned has a private office."

"Yes, Halle, he does and he worked here six years before he got one. In fact, his cubicle used to be down the hall about three cubes from where yours is now. So I have to tell you that I think your expectations are premature. You need to focus on developing real skills and increasing your depth of expertise in the field of HR rather focusing on job titles and promotions, much less private offices. Those may come with time, but it won't be for quite a while." Then I politely ended the meeting and sent her back to her cubicle.

We are not born with an entitlement mentality. That is acquired, whether from parents, our peers, society at large, the media, or from wherever; and once we have developed that mindset it is very hard to displace it. Those who are enmeshed with that outlook often display the following attitudes:

- What have you done for me lately? (Nothing you can do is ever enough.)
- Why can't I have what I want right now? (Instant gratification is their trademark.)

By contrast, some employees have expectations that are far too low or even non-existent. They sometimes muddle through the years of their employment never quite reaching that next level. This is not to say that everyone should aspire to a vertical promotion. In fact, often the highest level of job satisfaction that I observed was enjoyed by someone who was a subject-matter-expert. He or she was an individual contributor in whatever position they held, but usually everyone in their unit knew they were the go-to person for in-depth job knowledge.

Whether it was mechanical, mathematical, relational, or something else entirely, these motivated individuals were not drawn to the vertical ladder of job promotion. This is why compensation and career planning experts developed what are known as dual-ladder career paths. If one had no desire for promotions into management, they could still pursue promotion through a technical track, suited to their skills. For such individuals, their satisfaction came from knowing the ins and outs, the subtly obscure, but uniquely valuable, aspects of their job. I always held such individuals in high regard. Usually so did everyone else.

However, for the person who wanted to achieve promotional advancement but had not been able to figure out how to do that, I sometimes had the good fortune to mentor or coach them. Calvin was one such employee. He presented at my office one fall afternoon, looking sharp but wearing a somewhat glum expression. I knew he had just recently applied for a promotion and had not been selected, so I understood he was probably a little discouraged.

"Hi, Calvin. Come on in. I'm glad you called. How is your day going?"

"Good, good. I'm looking forward to our discussion. I have to tell you I'm a little nervous, though. I've never done anything like this. You know just decide to step forward."

"Well, I'm glad you decided to do some exploration and I will do everything I can to assure that your time is not wasted."

For the next hour or so Calvin told me about his tenure with the company, which departments he had worked in, what his specific job skills were, and what he wanted to do with them. During that time, I asked him a series of questions designed to identify what his personal strengths were and what his roadblocks seemed to be, that is what was hindering him from getting to where he wanted to go. Essentially it boiled down to this – he had been with the company for about eighteen years and he had never gotten a promotion. He had received good evaluations and decent raises and he and his manager got along well together. But anytime an opening for a supervisory position came along, Calvin just never got the nod. He could not figure it out. He was pretty sure he was well-liked among his crew and he knew that his boss respected his work. It was a mystery to him. I took a lot of notes during this initial meeting and Calvin left with a job-related questionnaire to fill out and bring back to me at our next session.

Over the next several months, Calvin and I met once a week to talk about risk/reward scenarios and to game plan for the next promotional opening that might become available. One of the first questions I asked Calvin during our second coaching session was this: What have you done in the past two years on "your own time and your own dime" to enhance your job skills or your value to the company? He offered that he had attended a couple of all-day training sessions a few months ago, which were put on by the company and were voluntary attendance. He was one of only two guys in his unit that chosen to go.

"That's good, but you said it was on company time so you were being paid to be there, even if you were not required to be there. Right? What I am talking about is anything you have done that was outside your work hours, on your own time, and for which you were not being paid. In fact, the kind of career enhancement effort I am referring to may cost you some money that is not reimbursable by the company. So your dime. See what I mean? Have you done anything like that?"

Calvin looked a little startled and said that he had never even thought about it. "Well, think about it," I advised him. "That is your assignment for next week. Find something that is work related, but it does not have to be directly related to your current position, and which you can only do on 'your own time and your own dime.' Let me know what you find out."

The following week, Calvin brought me a brochure on a seminar scheduled for the next Saturday. This was being offered at a nearby community college on a technical aspect of services similar to some of those our company offered. These were handled in an area in which he had never worked. It cost about a hundred dollars and would take about eight hours to attend. I encouraged him to do it and to be sure to get either a certificate of completion or to bring back some of the materials from the seminar for our next meeting. I think he thought it was my way of checking up on him, but it was not.

That next week, Calvin arrived for our meeting and enthusiastically shared some of what he had learned with me. I asked him about the certificate of completion or any materials he might have. He pulled a certificate out of his bag and laid it on the table, but he looked a little disappointed, as though he thought maybe I didn't believe he had actually attended the event.

"Great. Now here is what this is for, Calvin. First, I am going to make a copy of this and place it in your personnel file. Did you realize that managers often review an employee's file before they write their annual evaluation or decide upon a pay raise? Managers each have quite a number of subordinates and they can't be expected to remember what each employee has done during the entire year, so this is one way they refresh their view of the person's performance. More importantly for your purposes, any manager or director considering someone for promotion is going to request the employee's personnel file. And here will be evidence that you have taken some personal initiative to enhance your value to the company.

Secondly, I want you to make another copy of the certificate, and one or two pages of the material and put them in your manager's in-box along with a quick note saying something like, 'Just wanted you to know what I've been learning. Let me know if you have any questions for me about this.' This will put it right in front of his eyes and will cause him to recognize that you have done something above and beyond what was required. Managers tend to remember things like that. Then if another manager says, 'I've got an opening coming up for a supervisory position in my department. Anyone in your group that stands out?' you may be the guy he thinks of to recommend for an interview."

Now Calvin grinned at me and said, "Thanks. I didn't realize. I guess I thought as long as I showed up and did my job well, that was enough."

"It is enough, Calvin. It is just not enough to get you promoted. Not usually anyway." Then I asked him when was the last time he worked overtime that was needed but was not mandatory. Again, he hesitated and admitted it had been a while. After all, he had over fifteen years on the job and when urgent overtime was called for the newer guys usually ended up having to work it.

"Well, Calvin, I would like you to consider this if you want to lead others. An effective leader never asks anyone else to do something he or she is not willing to do themselves. Required overtime often means there is a problem or an issue that needs special attention. Because you are skillful with lots of experience, having you there when a situation like that occurs could help some of the younger or newer guys have a chance to learn from you. And maybe everybody gets the job done a little faster and gets to go home to dinner a little sooner. Leadership is not about having the newest work truck among the crew or the best set of tools, it is about being of value to those you work with and about being available when they can benefit from your expertise."

A few months later Calvin got an internal interview for a promotion. There were six applicants, four external and two internal. Once again, he did not get the job, but at my suggestion he went back to the hiring director, a week after the decision had been announced, to ask a couple of questions. Were there gaps in his skills or experience that he could shore up to better position himself for the next opening? Was there anything the director could point out that Calvin could have done better on during the interview? I knew this was a hard assignment. But by now, I also knew that it was exactly this kind of pro-active effort that was lacking in Calvin's career history. I also knew that he was serious about wanting to move ahead so this was to his benefit, if he could bring himself to ask for difficult feedback.

The director gave Calvin some good information and one encouraging piece of news that he did not ask for. After answering Calvin's questions honestly and fully, the director had volunteered to Calvin, "You know I am glad to get this chance to go over this with you. I think you might want to know that you came in second for the position. The guy we chose had more specific technical experience than you have, but you have more institutional knowledge than he has. So hang in there. I think you have what it takes."

Not quite a year later, Calvin again put in for a promotion. I will never forget the light in his eyes and the excitement in his voice when he stopped by my office just before quitting time to tell me, "Marsha, guess what? I got it! I got the job." Hearty handshakes and a "good for you" and we both went home smiling. I really did love this work of tending people.

Tending Tip:
- Youthful inexperience is one thing. But an exaggerated sense of one's own importance is quite another and should be nipped in the bud whenever possible.
- There are very few things on the job that can give you real joy more than that of helping someone else achieve their own goal. To be able to show someone how to add value, rather than simply act important, is a privilege.

Chapter Sixteen

LET THE GOOD TIMES ROLL

Comedy movies often show employees behaving outrageously at the notorious company holiday party because they had imbibed one, or a dozen, too many. I had on more than one rueful occasion had to be the company representative facing such an employee across the desk the following Monday morning; trying to determine whether their behavior warranted suspension, demotion, termination, or none of the above, in light of their actions. Was anyone injured? Had damage been done? Had confidential information been divulged? Were we facing litigation from anyone as result of their misconduct? And on and on. Oh, sure, just let the good times roll.

It was the worst sexual harassment case I ever encountered in all my years in corporate life. The Carpenters sang about "rainy days and Mondays always get me down." Talk about knowing their stuff. I walked in that Monday with no idea of the deluge of bad news that was about to greet me.

I had always made it a habit to clear my desk before leaving the office on Friday evening. This was partially due to the fact that more than half of the documents I dealt with were confidential and had to be kept under lock and key. But it was also due to the fact Monday mornings were less stressful when greeted by a shining – uncluttered – desk top. I just never subscribed to the old bumper-sticker that "If a cluttered desk reflects a cluttered mind, then an empty desk suggests an empty mind." Just not buying it.

So I was immediately on alert when I waltzed in, cheerful as a little bluebird, to spot a whole stack of papers topped off with a sealed manila envelope on my desk. I was certain none of that had been there when I left Friday afternoon. As I began to quickly leaf through the papers, I discovered that there were no fewer than five signed complaint statements from individual female employees, topped off by a sixth in the sealed envelope. It was sealed because it contained pictures to accompany the complaint – pictures of bruises and scrapes the employee stated she had received in a wrestling match with her boss, Leonard, the director of sales, over the weekend, while on a company sponsored event involving a chartered bus trip. He had – allegedly – attempted to visit his attentions upon her and had become fairly irate when she resisted.

I thought to myself, quite unprofessionally, no wonder she resisted. He is thirty years older than she is and has all the personality of a block of cement. Leonard was in his late fifties, a tall thin man with iron grey hair who usually wore an iron-grey expression. His stoic and self-righteous demeanor had always struck me as out of character for a salesman. Whether men or women, the sales folks were usually gregarious hail-fellow-well-met types in my experience. But then again, I had only been around this director when he was sober, and all six complainants asserted that he had been, not to put too fine a point on it, drunk as a skunk by the time these events occurred. And here was the kicker. Not only were six different employees making nearly identical complaints, this had all reportedly transpired in full view of around two dozen other employees. Wait. What?

As I sat down – hard – at my desk, my phone rang and the caller display indicated it was the assistant sales director, Jake, calling. His boss, Leonard, was the man against whom the allegations were being directed and I could only assume Jake, as Leonard's number two guy, was calling me to try to get ahead of the coming storm. Not exactly. Jake was calling to basically confirm the reports, and to add that he himself had practically had to carry his inebriated "superior" to his hotel room and tuck him in as Leonard was passed out cold by the time they reached his room.

Jake was one of the good guys in this business: he was professional, friendly, respectful and good at his job. He was also deeply embarrassed about what his boss had done over the weekend and yet, felt sorry for him, too. Was Leonard going to be fired? That was his first question. I told him that I had only seen the complaints two minutes ago and could not even begin to tell him how this would all play out. However, if the allegations proved to be true (I didn't mention the photos to Jake) then it was pretty much a foregone conclusion that, yes, Leonard would be fired. Jake said he was afraid that was the likely outcome and wanted me to know that he was in complete support of the women who had submitted complaints, and he would do all he could to cooperate with the company's investigation of the matter. He added that the whole thing was just crazy, because Leonard had always told him that he didn't drink, at all. Period. Furthermore, prior to this fiasco, Jake had never seen Leonard pick up a drink either on or off duty and they had worked together for some time.

The investigation took four weeks, and in the process of conducting it I learned more than I ever wanted to know about the lives of those involved. This was the HR equivalent of trench warfare and I was wading through the "mud and the blood and the beer" (as Johnny Cash sang in A Boy Named Sue.) I interviewed all six women that same Monday, one after the other, and dragged myself home late that evening feeling like I had been run over by that stupid charter bus where this all began!

There were several reasons for speaking with each of them on the same day. First, I wanted them to know that their complaint was being taken seriously and acted upon immediately. And I wanted to meet with each of them on the same day, so that no one was relegated to "day two" and feel that she was somehow less important or that her safety was secondary to anyone else's. Secondly, I wanted to offer them counseling from any counselor they chose, paid for by the company. Thirdly, on the extremely unlikely chance that this was somehow not what it seemed to be, I did not want to give them an opportunity to get together and "get their stories straight." They had arrived home Sunday evening from this event and this was the next morning–I wanted to hear their accounts fresh and, hopefully, without influence one upon another.

Each of their accounts was consistent with the others, but not identical. A couple of them had not been seriously accosted, but had been insulted. According to their accounts Leonard had attempted to pat or pet them. They were furious and wanted him fired – yesterday! He had tried to hug and kiss three of them, and had made inappropriate comments to them of a sexual nature. They were equally disgusted. And the sixth was the woman whose husband had taken pictures of her bruises as soon as she arrived home.

That was assault and my first question to her, after expressing my apologies and regret that such a thing had happened on a company sponsored outing, was had she notified the police, and/or did she want to? She told me that she and her husband had discussed it at length the night before, and they had decided that while they did not wish to involve the police at this time, they were prepared to do so if the company did not respond appropriately. (Good to know.) They were crystal clear that she was to come home immediately after her interview that day and would not be returning to work until he had been fired. (Understood.)

To my utter amazement, when I first interviewed Leonard he tried to brush the whole thing off as a little incident, insignificant really, that had happened over the weekend and really was not any of our business. I pointed out that it occurred on a company-sponsored road trip to reward the sales team for an outstanding year, and that the entire weekend's expenses had been paid for by the company. That made it our business. Furthermore, that did not begin to address the fact that I had six employee complaints on my desk against him, personally and specifically. What I did not say to Leonard, but I certainly asked my own boss was, what had the company been thinking when they authorized this debacle? I mean, let's review.

The event had involved a chartered bus from Sacramento over the hills and through the woods to the Napa Valley. Some twenty-five to thirty employees were being rewarded for delivering sales results that were the best in many years. Quite a lot of celebratory sipping had gone on during the long bus trip. The destination was – wait for it – the Napa Wine Train, a tourist destination that was well-known for attracting visitors from far and wide. As one might guess from the name of the attraction, wine was also served during the train ride, right after wine had been consumed on the three hour bus ride. What could possibly go wrong?

We were dealing with six understandably shaken employees. Their complaints met every classic definition of sexual harassment: the behavior was unwelcome, the alleged perpetrator was their superior in the workplace, which gave him power over their employment, and they had each attempted to tell him "no" and he had ignored them. There was no history or implication that any of the six women had ever been involved with Leonard in anything other than a professional capacity. Finally, none of the six had ever before filed a complaint of harassment, not that doing so would have negated this complaint, but it might have cast a shadow upon it. There was such a thing as the overly-sensitive, or serial complainer who, when denied the assignment or promotion he or she desired, suddenly lodged a harassment complaint. Such complaints also had to be investigated, unraveled, and documented with all due consideration. But, no, this was a complex and unmitigated disaster.

To merge and summarize their accounts of what happened, here is the recap: Upon reaching Napa, the group departed the bus, not a few already a little tipsy, but Leonard even a little more so. They boarded the Napa Wine Train where more bottles of wine, along with beautiful trays of fruit and cheese and crackers were also provided. Their group filled one entire car of the train and a few had to sit in a second car. Still, most of them were all aboard the same car. Leonard was seated near the back of that car, purportedly with his own bottle. Shortly he began to wander up and down the aisle, making questionable remarks and jokes. People began to get a little nervous. Then he attempted to sit with several of the younger women, and after joining them uninvited, he put his arm along the back of the seat and then started to squeeze their shoulders. One or two got up and moved to a different seat.

When they reached one of the stops on the tour, a female employee attempted to pass Leonard on her way out of the car. He grabbed the scarf she was wearing around her neck and used it to draw her to him as he tried to kiss her. She called out to one of the guys exiting the car, who looked back and immediately came back and told Leonard to "knock it off." By this time Leonard was so drunk that he could barely stand up, so he just shrugged and sat back down.

When the group re-boarded the train a few minutes later, Leonard again tried to accost that same lady. She tried to avoid him, but a train car aisle doesn't allow much room for maneuvering. He caught her arm, spun her around, grabbed her by both arms and kissed her loudly on the mouth, while she tried to wriggle out of his grasp. He had tightened his grip on both arms, and that created the dark bruises which her husband had taken photos of when she arrived home the following day. She also had faint bruising on her neck from where he had tightened the scarf after grabbing it to pull her to him. These were the photos on my desk the following Monday morning.

All of this occurred in the presence of nearly twenty coworkers, only two or three of which made any attempt to stop what was happening. Leonard was, after all, their boss. Most chose to ignore it and pretend it wasn't happening. The train trip was followed by a further jaunt on the chartered bus, down to a hotel in San Francisco, where the group was feted during an elegant dinner theater show. They spent Saturday night at the hotel and took the bus home the next day.

Astonishingly, Leonard refused to take any responsibility for what had happened. And he had concocted a bizarre story about why it had occurred. He claimed that he had consumed some shell fish which, combined with the wine, had produced an allergic reaction along the lines of a psychedelic episode. This had caused him to behave in an uncharacteristically aggressive manner. In other words, this was all due to a medical issue beyond his control. (No one else recalled any shell fish being served on the train.) He had also retained an attorney. While the company decided to let the lawyers and the doctors sort that one out, in HR we began to lay the groundwork for terminating his employment, based upon the six verified complaints.

Weeks later, I was tasked with calling Leonard at home (he had not been allowed back on company property since the episode) to ask him to meet with all parties involved; his boss, the attorneys (his and ours), my boss, and me to discuss how to resolve this matter. Leonard was not home and I spoke briefly with his wife, who seemed puzzled as to why I would be calling him at home in the middle of the work day. I simply told her that there must be some misunderstanding and politely ended the call.

It turned out that he had been putting on a suit, taking his briefcase, and going to a local library each day for nearly a month, rather than tell his wife what had happened and why he was not at work. I strongly suspected that this was not the first time Leonard had derailed his employment with out-of-control drinking. It explained the severely restrained manner he had always previously displayed, and the fact that he had told Jake that he did not drink; in contrast to his flagrant actions once he began drinking the day of the bus trip. He sounded to me very much like what is known as a "dry drunk" – someone for whom drinking is supposedly a thing of the past, but who is often right on the precipice of falling off the wagon. Generally if such a person does pick up a drink, what follows is an inevitable disaster.

But I was no rehab counselor, so what did I know? I did know that I had six employees who were justified in thinking that they should not have to deal with this kind of behavior on the job. I had attorneys telling me the liability to the company, if we kept him on, was enormous. And I had an offender who showed no contrition for the harm he had caused; but only offered up excuses that did not make a lot of sense. In my view, he had to go.

Just like the case itself, the settlement meeting was the worst I ever attended. In addition to the attorneys around the conference table (and more than one was always too many as far as I was concerned), two company executives, plus my boss and me, there was also a surprise attendee. Leonard had brought his wife to the meeting. She appeared to be in her fifties, an elegantly attractive woman, who was beautifully groomed wearing a stylish moss green dress and matching jacket, accessorized with a single strand of what looked like good quality pearls. Although her manner was sedate, her intelligent eyes as she took in the room and its occupants told me that she was perceptive. We were the antithesis of a cheerful gathering as we each took our places at the table.

It quickly became apparent as to why Leonard had brought his wife, Tamara, to the meeting. He hoped that by having her there, we would be unwilling or too squeamish to lay out the full facts. His attorney pressed us hard, asserting that as Leonard's employer we were obligated to take his "medical condition" into account. There was no real medical evidence presented, however, that explained Leonard's actions and he had never previously indicated that he had a propensity toward extreme allergic reactions of any kind. There was simply one written statement from one physician, who stated that such a thing was possible. Not that it had necessarily occurred in this instance, but that it was simply within the realm of possibility.

His attorney also claimed that he had a verbal employment contract that we would be breaking if he was terminated and that, at a minimum, we would owe him severance pay. Again, Leonard maintained he had done nothing amiss other than to suffer an unanticipated medical episode.

We pressed back, eventually having no choice but to disclose the worst details of his behavior, declaring that at least one instance constituted assault. As I was required to read from some of the most painful of the interviews, his wife maintained a stoic expression throughout; but again her eyes revealed more than she intended. Tamara looked like someone accustomed to handling banked rage and she did not appear to be fooled by his protestations of innocence.

Two hours later an agreement had been reached that made no one happy. This is usually one of the hallmarks of an effective compromise agreement – no one gets exactly what they hoped for, but everyone walks away with something. Rather than become involved in a protracted legal battle the company agreed to pay Leonard a modest severance, in exchange for his resignation. Bottom line – Leonard no longer worked for us.

Tending Tip:
- Due to such antics as those just described, some companies no longer serve alcohol at company sponsored functions. If they do, they maintain a strict drink limit, such as two drinks per person. It not only helps protect against host-liability, but helps assure no one's career gets derailed at such an event. If asked to weigh in, I encourage you to whole-heartedly support such limitations, if only to save yourself a boat load of work in the long run.
- Keep in mind, just because something sounds preposterous, that does not necessarily mean that it did not happen. However, this does not mean that you must believe the patently ridiculous.

Chapter Seventeen
More Good Times ... Or Something

A young trainee, Jesse, had quickly become an office favorite both for his winsome personality and for his gift of being able to diagnose and resolve almost any computer network related problem quickly and with a minimum of fuss. He had only been with us for about three months when the holiday party was held. He was very young, just barely of legal drinking age, and because he reported directly to me, (and I had heard Monday morning tales of his weekend exploits) I called him into my office the Friday evening before the party. He brought along a departmental buddy of his, Brett, who was equally smart, talented, and occasionally idiotic.

"Gentlemen," I began with what I hoped was a friendly smile, "Are you both planning to come to the holiday party?"

They both quickly assured me that they were looking forward to it. They were entry-level employees, and therefore did not often have a chance to bring a date to a soiree' at one of the upscale hotels in the city on the company tab. So I had the corporate equivalent of the "Mom-talk" with them, telling them to remember that although they would not be on the clock, they would still be among their co-workers and company executives. I encouraged them to have a good time, but to also remember not to do anything that could put their employment in jeopardy. They were both nice young men and they did me a kindness by refraining from rolling their eyes – at least while they were still in my office.

But youth and free drinks are a bad combination and the nearly inevitable happened. Jesse had a great time. However, others decided they were not having such a great time in proximity to where he was becoming louder and more out-of-control as the evening wore on. Throw in a couple of inappropriate jokes with sexual harassment implications written all over them, and come Monday morning – there we were; with Jesse on the wrong side of my desk, looking decidedly the worse for wear and wearing a hang-dog expression.

After reviewing all the facts, and keeping in mind his brief tenure, youthful ignorance, and genuinely remorseful apology, we managed to salvage his job, barely. He lost two-day's pay, and was put on probation for a few months. He later told me, "It was sort of worth it, to learn that lesson so early in my career." I could respect that.

In that particular case, there had not been any harassment, just some youthful stupidity. It could have been a lot worse.

I have seen love-sick notes from one co-worker to another who did not wish to receive them. I once dealt with a fellow who left a bouquet of dead, black roses on a female co-worker's chair, to try to convince her that he was "dead serious" about wanting to go out with her. She did not appreciate this romantic gesture, and we told him that if he approached her again we would have to fire him.

I have had occasion to play back voice mails to another offender, who steadfastly maintained he had not harassed *anyone,* much less the complainant, despite the twenty-two messages he had left on her voicemail, and regardless of her continued resistance to his attentions. And there was the female executive who was sued by a former director, who was her subordinate, who alleged that she had coerced him to have an affair with her in order for him to get a promotion. There was enough evidence to suggest that he was telling the truth that the company settled out of court on that one, although I was not personally involved in the case and only heard about it afterward from colleagues. Suffice it to say, the permutations of what was and was not harassment were endless.

However, my experience was that at least some of the time, there truly was no intent to harass someone or to make them uncomfortable. Sometimes there had been a misunderstanding between two individuals, who later recalled the details of an incident or former relationship differently. One of the most misunderstood issues in the workplace, sexual harassment allegations have been known to ruin a person's career, male or female, and like most HR professionals, I did not like having to address such issues. The only way to proceed, as far as I was concerned, was to take everyone at their word, unless and until, subsequent testimony and a preponderance of evidence proved them false.

No matter how diligently we worked to assure that there was a level playing field in the manner in which harassment complaints were handled, there were clear differences in the manner in which men and women usually approached the issue of sexual harassment. This is not the politically correct thing to say these days, but in my two decades of experience in dealing with such matters first hand, I can only attest that it is true.

Men, more often than not assumed that their career was automatically ruined, even for being accused, regardless of whether the allegation was substantiated. They further assumed that they would not be given a fair hearing on the allegations. However, in my years of dealing with such issues, my experience was that a substantial number of such complaints turned out to be unfounded or based upon a mutual misunderstanding. Contrary to popular rumors, it was a rare occurrence to see someone lose their job over a harassment complaint.

Women generally had a different attitude, namely that they would not be believed, that their complaint would be dismissed out of hand, often to the detriment of their standing in the workplace. Additionally, women, often with good reason, feared retaliation for having made a complaint and it was part of my job to assure that this did not occur.

When there was genuine sexual harassment discovered, it often had less to do with lust, and more to do with power and control. Occasionally there was a set of such convoluted circumstances that no amount of hard work, good intentions, or careful adherence to the guidelines, could resolve the matter. When the wife worked in cubicle five on the west side of the office, and the girlfriend worked in cubicle sixteen on the east side of the same office, and the husband/boyfriend worked somewhere in the middle of the whole mess, well, there was just no predicting how it would all work out.

Shouting matches, cat-fights, and tires with the air let out of them were not unknown. On days like those, which were thankfully rare, I went home asking myself why I ever went into human resources; because clearly it was a fool's errand.

It was my further experience that tenure and rank had no bearing upon how foolishly an individual might behave. One executive I questioned freely admitted that he had used company funds to pay for a supposed public relations / marketing calendar. The fact that said calendar contained a dozen (one per month) full-page, living color shots of his favorite assistant astride a motorcycle, clothed in as little as possible, seemed to him to have no bearing upon the matter. I personally could not help but wonder how she peeled herself off of all that leather, being glued to it by so much bare skin, without sustaining severe chafing. However, I admit that it was just passing curiosity, because I really did not care whether her skin remained intact after participating in such a dim-witted stunt. Shortly thereafter, she left the company to pursue her dream of becoming a fashion model.

Upon further investigation, it turned out that several hotel bills, restaurant tabs, etc., had also been rung up while Mr. Big Shot entertained female subordinates on the company dime. Only after several months of such antics, was he finally dismissed. And sadly, this was not strictly because of his inappropriate behavior and violation of company policy, but more because some of the senior executives became embarrassed by his behavior. He had become something of a public joke and that reflected poorly upon the organization's reputation.

At such times, the human resources professional is well-advised to keep in mind that we are not there to act as the company's moral police; however tempting that might be. We are there to assure that each employee has an opportunity to do his or her job free of harassment or undue pressure. It is a challenging line to walk. The issue must remain whether or not company policies have been violated, and/or whether any employee's rights have been ignored, rather than whether the HR person is offended. It did, however, sometimes make one long for the good old days when some employment contracts contained clauses about moral turpitude and the like. I had never actually seen such a contract, but I would have liked to have had one handy on more than one occasion.

Tending Tip:
- Never assume the guilt or innocence of anyone involved in a sexual harassment complaint. It may or may not turn out to be a legitimate complaint. Be cautious about early conclusions arrived at too easily; but also be prepared to be persuaded by the weight of the evidence.
- Do not allow the gender, age, length of service, job title, or any other attribute of the complainant to bias your outlook or your approach to dealing with the issue. The same applies to the person against whom the complaint is made. Focus on the company policies which are asserted to have been violated. Respect everyone's rights and protect everyone's confidentiality to the extent possible.
- Gather as much relevant information as possible, while also keeping the "need to know" circle as small as possible. And remember, not everyone who wants to know needs to know.

When necessary, and there will be such times, remind yourself that you did not make this mess; you are simply trying to clean it up with the least amount of damage possible.

Chapter Eighteen
Weep With Those Who Weep

The compensation team in my department was made up of individuals who were usually a fairly stoic bunch. They were as friendly and skillful as the other teams, but their jobs mostly involved numbers rather than people. Generally I could expect their work area to be a drama-free zone and I appreciated that about them. However, I walked into their work area one day to discover sad faces all around and one of them, Patricia, was in tears. She had just received the results of some medical tests on her daughter's condition and the news was not good.

Over the next year, we worked with her to accommodate chemotherapy schedules, surgery absences, and did whatever else we could to support her while her daughter slowly slipped away. She died just before her sixteenth birthday. I remember standing at the graveside and praying with Patricia and her family. They were broken and bowed, but they were still gracious as they invited a group of us back to their home after the services.

Much as in general life, we cannot always anticipate when grief will enter the workplace. In Patricia's case we had seen it coming and had some time to prepare for it. But that is not often the case. There was the time when a local sheriff's deputy came to my office to ask where he might be able to find one of our employees, Roberta. She worked in another building nearby, and I offered to escort him there. He said he appreciated it because he had come to deliver some very hard news and he did not want to do it alone. Roberta's brother's body had been discovered earlier that morning on a park bench in the city and he was there to do the family notification.

I did not personally know Roberta, but I could sit with her and listen. I could speak gently during those first terrible moments. Her brother had been homeless for several years and this was news the family had been dreading would come their way for a long time We could offer her flexibility, and some compassion, in how she wanted to handle that day and the coming days. It was the least we could do.

And perhaps one of the saddest days of all, at least in my years in the workplace, was the day one of our outside plant employees fell from several stories up, to his death. That day I saw men still wearing their tool belts wandering the hallways with blank stares on their faces, not even aware that there were tears running down their cheeks. It was gut-wrenching and we immediately called in a team of grief counselors to be available to our people. These are just a few examples of the many ways in which grief can impact the workplace and its people.

How does the human resources professional deal with the deep and tragic grief that can, and inevitably will, invade the workplace on any given day? I don't know that there is any one right answer to this question. But I do know this. HR people tend to want to fix things, as soon as possible. We people-tenders are "fixers" by nature. It is our temperament–practically in our DNA.

But we can't fix death. We cannot manage grief into compliance and we cannot motivate someone out of it. All we can do is to grieve with those who grieve, and yes, sometimes simply "weep with those who weep." (Romans 12:15 NKJV) We can show compassion and flexibility toward them as they deal with the worst day – or month – or year of their lives. Certainly, we can send food and flowers and cards. But more than that, we can be aware of how raw they feel and refrain from intruding further into their grief when they return from bereavement leave. We can behave with some sensitivity, without tiptoeing around them, which can make them more uncomfortable than they already are, especially during their first few days back at work.

To get up, put on your work clothes (whether that is a khaki uniform or a tailored suit) pick up your tools, or your briefcase, and head back into the fray after confronting the death of a loved one or the loss of a coworker is one of the hardest things most of us will ever have to do. Patricia, whose daughter died, called me the day before she was scheduled to return from her leave of absence. She had been gone about a month, but she needed to get back to work, and we were looking forward to having her back. However, she had a request.

She hoped it wasn't inappropriate, she said, but she wanted me to let the department know two things: first, she truly appreciated everything each one had done to help and support her; and secondly, she really did not want to be asked "how are you doing?" – "are things getting better?" – nor to be asked any other emotionally laden question. She thought she would be able to keep it together and get through these next few weeks – or months – if she could just be allowed to try to get back into her routine. Questions about how she was faring, even those that were well intentioned, were going to derail her, she admitted. I told her I would let the staff know about her specific request.

Grief is such a deeply personal thing, and it is sometimes the complete opposite of what we want to project in the workplace, which is confidence and competence. In order to maintain our equilibrium, we strive for depersonalization or compartmentalization of our lives, especially when we are hurting at home and trying to function at work. It isn't possible, of course, not all the time in every situation. But it is possible to give the grief-stricken employee some space, some time, some air when they first return to work. Pain is private and personal, particularly the pain of death. Walking the line, between feeling what we feel and doing what we are being paid to do, is sometimes daunting and never more so than when we are grieving.

The most difficult challenge I ever encountered, regarding this area of HR management, involved an employee who could not get past his own grief. Josh, a downline member of my own staff, lost his brother in a violent murder, during Josh's employment with our company. He was understandably devastated. As he requested, we approved a leave of absence, (LOA) and when he was unable to return at the end of that time, we approved an extension. After he had exhausted all accrued paid leave, we continue to approve unpaid leave while holding his job for him.

After several months he finally returned to his job. He seemed okay at first. He showed up on time and went through the routines of his day fairly normally. He was subdued, of course, and no one thought less of him for the struggle he was obviously still having in trying to cope with what had happened. However, more than a year after the crime occurred (and after the perpetrator had been caught and jailed) I began to receive phone calls from other departmental managers.

"Marsha you are going to have to talk to Josh. I know he suffered a terrible loss, but he is really beginning to bother some of the employees in my department. He sits in the break room and corners anyone he can and talks endlessly about his brother's gruesome murder. It is really starting to creep some of them out. Could you talk to him? I know it won't be easy, but this can't continue."

So I reluctantly called Josh into my office and we talked about how he was doing and whether there was anything we could do to further support his recovery. He had let us know that he was regularly seeing a grief counselor and he was also in a support group, so there was little else I could offer in the way of resources. Things seemed better for a couple of weeks and then I got another call, and then a third one.

Lester, a director in another area of the company, called one evening and he was exasperated. It seemed Josh had been working with one of the supervisors in Lester's downline to assist in developing a PIP (performance improvement plan) for an employee. However, Lester said, "Josh keeps derailing the process by insisting on rehashing the details of his brother's murder. Gordy, the supervisor, was sympathetic at first, but now he is getting uncomfortable hearing it over and over. He is sorry it happened, we all are. But we are running a business here not a grief center and this has got to stop."

I apologized on behalf of my subordinate and assured Lester that I would address this right away. I called Harry, Josh's supervisor, who reported to me. Harry and I had a lengthy discussion about what to do and frankly we were stumped. The next day the three of us (Josh, Harry and I) sat down in my office to … to do what? Fix the problem? Fix Josh? What exactly was the answer here? Neither Harry nor I had been able to come up with a workable solution, although we had given it some serious consideration. This meeting was to be one of those rare encounters where the agenda was unclear and the outcome was completely uncertain. This problem was intractable and the way forward was shrouded in confusion.

We began the meeting by asking Josh how he was doing, and he replied, "Okay, I guess." Then, as sensitively as we knew how, we explained to him that we had received some concerning reports about his interactions with people in other departments. We again acknowledged that he and his family had been through a terrible ordeal and we truly sympathized. However, we said, we were concerned about the path he seemed to be on. Josh immediately became defensive asking whether someone had complained about him and asking what was he supposed to do, just pretend his brother hadn't been killed.

The next hour was painful and stressful – for all three of us. Harry explained to Josh that for the last three months he had been assigning work "around Josh" – partly in order to allow him space to recover while he worked. But, Harry continued, part of the work-around was because other supervisors and managers were telling us that they were finding it difficult to work with him. Harry was circumspect and did not tell Josh that just that week a director had called HR for assistance on a personnel matter and had said, "Send anyone over you think can handle this ... that is, anyone but Josh. We just don't want to deal with him anymore. Enough is enough."

Now we had hit critical mass. Even those in the workforce with a severe disability (which obviously included Josh at this point) according to the Americans with Disabilities Act of 1990 (ADA) had to be willing and able to perform their duties with any necessary and reasonable accommodation. We had done everything we knew to do to accommodate Josh in his grief recovery process. But it had been about a year and he seemed to be stuck in the grief part, while there was little to no recovery happening, at least not where his work was concerned. I felt empathy for Josh and Harry did, too. But a number of his coworkers, even those who still empathized with him, were getting weary of carrying part of his workload plus their own.

So we let him know that we were sending him home for the rest of the day, not as any sort of discipline, but out of concern for him. We encouraged him to talk to a friend or family member, to take a long walk, or do anything that he felt might alleviate some of his stress. We would continue to work with him to the best of our ability, however, when he returned to work we wanted to be clear that his behavior would have to change. He could not continue to engage coworkers in lengthy discussions about his family's tragedy and he would need to begin to rebuild his workload. Not all at once, of course, but we would have to see some progress over the next month.

Josh left the meeting furious. I learned later that afternoon that he had immediately gone directly to a coworker, Wanda, and had given her his version of a blow-by-blow account of our earlier meeting with him. She was upset on his behalf and came to my office just before the end of the day to confront me about it. "If even half of what Josh told me you and Harry said to him this afternoon is true, then I am really disappointed in both of you. How can you do this to him? Where is your heart? I used to admire you, but now I am not only disappointed, I am disgusted with both of you." (Meaning me and Harry.)

I listened to all of this with a lump in my throat and then reminded Wanda that, as she well knew, any discussion I had with another employee about his or her performance was confidential and therefore, I could not discuss it with her. She then proceeded to tell me some of what she had heard from Josh. As I listened I was increasingly saddened and alarmed to realize that some of what he had told her was simply untrue. And most of the rest of it, he had twisted into an account wherein Harry and I had been callous and even unreasonable in what we had said. Wanda had just become collateral damage in Josh's misfortune. I wish I could say it was temporary, but it was not. From that day on Wanda was a resentful person to work with and the previously warm relationship we had always enjoyed was permanently damaged.

It further concerned me that if this was the way Josh was interacting with his own manger and department head, I could better understand how other directors and managers were now saying, "Don't send Josh over here. Send anyone but him." As Lester had said to me, this had to stop. I realized that there was no timeline in grief recovery, but there had to be a boundary in the workplace. Josh called in sick the following day. When he returned to work the day after that, he sat in his cubicle doing little other than answering a few emails. During that last month he was with us, he became increasingly hostile toward others, particularly if anyone disagreed with him. He could be overheard muttering, "You people just don't understand. You don't know what it is like."

After making one more attempt to get Josh to understand that his work was no longer acceptable and that, furthermore, his relationships with others in the work place were continuing to deteriorate, we were preparing to let him go when he resigned. We arranged for Josh to leave with as little awkwardness as possible, for his sake. Wanda again became angry with me because we did not have a good-bye luncheon for Josh. I could not even imagine how strained the conversations would have been around that table had such an event occurred. But there was no reasoning with her. As I watched him carry his box of belongings to his car, I stood at my window feeling completely defeated. I had seldom in my career felt like such a total failure. This was a problem that I could not fix.

Josh had so completely identified himself, first with the victim, and then ultimately as a victim himself, that he could not hear what we were saying to him. He could only lash out at anyone who tried to help and alienate anyone who could not continue to offer him a bottomless well of sympathy. Several years later I was watching the local evening news, and the story was about victims' rights. A group was holding a protest on the capitol steps to lobby for better funding for victim reparations and support. Suddenly the camera focused on a large sign being waived by someone I recognized – Josh. This had become his identity, his life's focus – victimhood. The reporter thrust the microphone into Josh's face, and I heard that once familiar voice begin to say, "People don't understand what it is like." I turned the program off.

Tending Tip:
- We try to avoid failure at all costs. But sometimes the cost of avoidance becomes too high. There may come a rare occasion when we simply have to accept it. We hear the phrase "failure is not an option." But sometimes it is the reality. Not every problem can be fixed, at least not in the workplace and not by HR. Accept the failure, but don't waste it. Learn from it.
- It may seem unfair and lacking in compassion to deal with a dysfunctional employee who can no longer perform the job. But it is even more unfair to expect his/her coworkers to carry that person's workload indefinitely. There must be a limit, a boundary, at some point. Identifying that point in time and having the courage to take action is painfully necessary. To refuse to do so is not kindness, it is avoidance.

Chapter Nineteen

THE SECRET STASH

My phone rang on a busy Wednesday afternoon and I answered with no clue as to how annoying, incredible, and downright absurd the next few moments would become. Of course my desk phone had a display allowing me to see who was calling, but I did not recognize the employee's name, and as far as I could recall, he had never before called me.

That was not unusual. Pareto's 80/20 principle was alive and operating at full capacity in our organization, as I suspect it does in most companies. Eighty percent of the employees caused only twenty percent of my work, but twenty percent of the employees created eighty percent of my problems.

This guy, Tyler, was an unknown quantity and I had no idea where he fit in the 80/20 rule. Just because I had never heard from him personally, did not mean that one or more members of my team had not perhaps interacted with him upon occasion. I made a mental note to check around after we finished the call. Still, I was not aware of anything major that was brewing, nothing that might cause me any undue concern as I answered with my typical, "Hello, this is Marsha."

"Marsha, this is Tyler over in IT services. I have a real problem and I want you to do something about it right away. It has been going on for a while now, and I need you to do something ASAP."

"Tyler, maybe you had better back up and begin at the beginning, because I have no idea what you are talking about. What has been going on and what is it that you need from me?"

Simply knowing that he was in information technology (IT) network services raised my level of concern, because when something went wrong with the network, or even a significant portion of it, we had bigger problems than any one employee. Customer service and public relations could quickly be negatively impacted causing a black eye for the whole enterprise. We prided ourselves on achieving and maintaining a better than ninety-nine percent reliability level. Given that we were a 24/7 operation, it was not easily done and any threat to that status was dealt with quickly and forcefully.

Nevertheless, at this point I did not know Tyler's specific area of responsibility and thus could not know whether he was working on the Local Area Network (LAN), the Wide Area Network (WAN), the major T1 transport lines, or something else. For all I knew, maybe he was a help desk person who had run afoul of an internal customer (a fellow employee) who was giving him grief. Instead of giving me some pertinent information, Tyler shocked me considerably by replying with a question of his own. "Could you come over here and dust my work area for fingerprints?"

"What? What are you talking about? First of all, we are not the HR police over here, Tyler. And secondly, why in the world do you think your work area needs to be dusted for fingerprints?"

"Well, something has been stolen, and I thought maybe you could help me get it back. You know, confidentially. I've heard you're pretty big on confidentiality over there in HR and that you personally handle some investigations. Isn't that true? If it is, then that is what I want. I want you to launch a confidential investigation. Will you do that?"

Now he had me intrigued, but also completely dumbfounded. I explained to him that the kind of "investigations" I and my team did generally had nothing to do with property theft, if that was what he meant by "something" had been stolen. I asked whether this was a theft of company equipment or personal property.

Our company dealt in some highly proprietary equipment, some of which was under patent protection. I could understand his near-panic if a critical piece of equipment, for which he was personally responsible, had gone missing. Very small items of a highly complex nature could be hand-carried out of the building, and we had recently had such a theft resulting in a loss of tens of thousands of dollars.

"Tyler, I need you to understand that if this is a serious theft, that is a criminal matter and I will need to notify the police immediately. We do not do that kind of investigation internally."

"No, no, no. That is not what I mean at all. Please do *not* call the police," he said emphatically. "I don't want to get the police involved in this. This is personal. I believe that another employee has been stealing from me. And it has happened more than once. That is why I am calling you. This is a coworker stealing from me. Are you sure you can't just dust for prints and figure out who is doing it?"

I tried to regather my rapidly waning patience and began to explain to Tyler that human resources, while there to serve employees, did not do criminal investigations. I further assured him that I did not now, nor had I ever, possessed a finger printing kit. Additionally, as he should know from his own experience, the company did not require finger prints on file, except for a very few highly sensitive positions. And because he was beginning to really annoy me with his odd combination of panic and stubborn resistance to providing any detail, I asked him another question. "Exactly what is it that you believe would have incriminating finger prints on it?"

"My desk area in my cubicle. Specifically the front of my desk drawers."

Recalling where Tyler worked, I pictured a standard two or three story cube-farm. His work area was large with forty or fifty separate work spaces designed from modular pieces, which could be reconfigured in a day or two to form new work arrangements whenever needed. There were no desks, as such, but rather modular work counters, and sliding door cubby holes for storage, etc. The raised cubicle "walls" generally were either four, five or six feet high. The drawers underneath the work surface were faced with either a subtle nubby fabric, or with a finely pebbled laminate of some kind.

"Okay. That would be a challenge even for the authorities and here is why. Your particular type of cubicle equipment has either a fabric or an uneven laminate surface, if I am recalling your building's cubicles and work spaces correctly. They do not have a smooth surface, except for your work surface, correct?"

"Well, yes. That is true."

"In light of that, I doubt they could retrieve any usable prints even if we asked them to; but as I said, I have no real experience in that area. You said this is personal, so may I ask, what is it that has gone missing?"

"Money" he replied tersely. "Quite a bit of money."

Now I was really irked.

"Tyler" I began, with no small amount of exasperation in my voice, "you know the company policy about keeping valuables in your work area. The handbook is pretty clear that employees are strongly urged to avoid keeping anything worth over about fifty dollars in their work area, even in a locker with a padlock, much less in a desk drawer."

"I realize that, but I really did not have any place else to keep it. I didn't want to leave it in my car, and I couldn't stash it at ...uh, well, I just didn't have any other place to keep it. So I have been keeping it in a locked drawer at my desk. I count it once a week, and keep certain amounts rolled and held with a rubber band."

Now I was aghast. How much money was he describing? Rolled bundles held by rubber bands? This was uncharted territory. "Good heavens, Tyler. How much money do you believe has been stolen?"

"Today, when I checked, I discovered the largest amount that had gone missing so far. It was just over a thousand dollars. It began with just a small amount missing several weeks ago. The first time I thought I noticed it, it was an odd amount of less than a hundred dollars. I thought maybe I had miscounted, when I put the money away the previous week. But the next time it was close to two hundred dollars and I was sure about the amount I had locked away the prior week. A couple of times after that it was two hundred each time, then over three hundred.

I usually stay a little late on the evening that I count it, and someone must have seen me counting it, even though I thought everyone else had left for the day. I've been looking around and trying to figure out who is doing this, but I just can't seem to identify whoever it is. Then yesterday, when I counted it, and realized how much was gone this time, I decided to call you."

I sat bemusedly with the phone in my hand, completely knocked back in my black leather, ergonomically designed chair. What in creation had this idiot been up to? I wasn't sure I even wanted to know; but I was too far into this mess to back out now.

"Tyler," I asked faintly, "how much money – all totaled – did you have locked in your desk drawer, when all this started?"

"Something over eleven thousand dollars," he replied matter-of-factly. Now I wanted to beat my own head with my stapler. Then I wanted to grab a post-it note and staple it to Tyler's forehead – with the word IDIOT written on it.

"And how much money has been stolen over these past weeks?"

Now it was his turn, apparently, to feel irked, because he had a certain tone in his voice as if I should have been able to figure this out by now. "Nearly two thousand dollars" he said bitterly.

"Tyler, if I am hearing you correctly, you have had over eleven thousand dollars locked in your desk area for some months now. Then a few weeks ago, perhaps as much as a couple of months, you began to notice that some of it was missing when you did your weekly count. Then yesterday, when you did your weekly count, you discovered that over a thousand dollars was gone. So you called me. Is that about right?"

"Yes," he said in a puzzled manner, as though he was speaking with someone who wasn't very quick on the uptake. "That's what I've been trying to tell you."

"Well, then I just have one question. Tyler, if you have known for weeks and weeks that money was being taken, stolen out of your desk, *why in the world didn't you remove it*?"

There was a pause as Tyler was apparently trying to figure out the simplest way to explain this to the person on the other end of the line; someone who clearly did not have great comprehension skills. "Because, Marsha, if I had done that, then *they would know I was onto them!*"

I could not possibly make this stuff up. On the off chance that he could figure out who was taking his money, Tyler had left it to be stolen repeatedly–for weeks. Who does that?

After a few further pithy instructions to him to get that money out of the office now – and never bring it back again, I hung up. As a friend of mine from the Midwest would have said, I was completely bumfuzzled. I did not know whether to wind the cat or put out the clock.

And then I began to laugh – and I laughed until my sides ached and my eyes were streaming. Two members of my staff put their heads into my office, looking at me as if to say, "Come on share the joke." I just waived them away and continued laughing.

I had offered, twice more before hanging up, to call the local police and help Tyler file a report on the thefts. He stoutly declined, saying he wanted to keep this private. I obtained his assurances that the money would be out of our building by end of business that day. Beyond that, my hands were tied.

It was obvious that the money was somehow illicit. Perhaps he had a gambling problem and this was his stake in the Saturday night game, kept at the office so the wife wouldn't know about it. Or maybe it was money he had earned on a side job and was not listing on his tax returns, or perhaps he was planning a couples-vacation where the wife was not the intended significant other. Whatever the reason for "the secret stash," he preferred to allow it to be stolen rather than "let them know" he was onto them. Herein lies a mystery. The folks we tend occasionally defy all logic as to their actions and motives.

Tending Tip: Try to do the right thing as often as you can figure out what that is. The rest of the time, have enough sense to steer clear of whatever else is going on. Good luck with that.

In any moment of decision, the best thing you can do is the right thing, the next best thing is the wrong thing, and the worst thing you can do is nothing."[14] ~ Theodore Roosevelt

Chapter Twenty
CLEVER BUT CLUELESS

A new member of the executive team had recently joined the company. He came to us with a European banking background to serve as our new Chief Marketing Officer (CMO). He was good-looking, debonair, and pretty impressive if he did say so himself – and he did. Noble (I think he chose his own name while still in the womb) swanned around for months, generally alienating everyone within earshot, although it wasn't his upper crust accent that especially annoyed them. They kind of got a chuckle out of that. No, the thing that got on everyone's nerves was his condescension toward anyone who did not have his international business experience. And that meant nearly all of our current executives and board members.

After several months of Noble's disdainful attitude, and his general lack of cooperation with others on the executive team, the CEO called me and said, "Marsha, I want you to meet with Noble and dial him down. The board is hearing rumbles about his negative interactions, and I'm not going to be able to keep him much longer, if he cannot make some necessary adjustments. Go see what you can do."

My jaw clenched at this directive as I thought about the fact that Noble was a high level acquisition who had been recruited by an outside search firm *and* he had been hired directly by the CEO. The firm our company employed to conduct this executive search was nationally known and enjoyed a solid reputation for good results. However, the "talent acquisition expert" (head-hunter) who worked this particular assignment knew little of our firm and virtually nothing of our corporate culture. Nevertheless, this firm had been handsomely paid to send Noble our way and it irritated me that the "claw-back period" had recently expired. (This was the agreed upon time frame during which some of head-hunter's fee – typically thirty-percent of the annual salary of the new hire–would be returned to us if that person did not work out.) With a self-righteous sigh, I went where I was told. Here I was, twenty-plus years down the road, still occasionally caught between the rock I did not know and the hard place I had not chosen.

By this time in my career I held the title of executive director. That meant I was operating not far below the "C-Suite" (CEO, COO, CFO, etc.), but after a few hard fought battles and more than a few organizational skirmishes, I also filled the unofficial role of executive coach. This role had evolved over a number of years, as various vice-presidents, directors and other management members sought me out to discuss some particularly thorny dilemma in their area of responsibility. I appreciated their confidence in me, and they had learned that they could depend upon my discretion.

Many companies hired outside consultants to coach or mentor executives through career challenges. However, our company's top two or three executives, as well as a couple of board members, had decided that I was just about as effective (at least as far as they could tell) as anyone they could hire from the outside, and I did not cost the company nearly as much per day. They really were too gracious. If it all went badly it might be my job on the line; whereas an outside consultant simply cashed the company's sizeable check and walked away. Such outside consultants were frequently booked months ahead, and if the problem was urgent, and in Noble's case it was rapidly becoming so, it was much more convenient to pick up the phone and summon me. (Truthfully, I suspected that on any given day it was about a toss-up as to whether it was my coaching ability or the cost-effectiveness of using me versus an outsider that was the deciding factor.)

At the time I was also completing a master's program, and was currently working on a case study about a European company for which, I had recently learned, Noble's prior banking employer had done some financing. I hoped this might give us something to talk about to break the ice.

I called Noble and set up a meeting, although he made it clear that it could not possibly happen sooner than the following week, because he had much higher level things to deal with than chatting with the HR director. Little did he know that I had both the CEO and the board's ear on this matter and that he had a lot more riding on our little chat than he realized. I didn't think it wise to mention that to him at that moment.

The following week we met in a conference room in the building where his office was located. He had suggested we meet in his office but I knew that, given his attitude, he wanted to be on his own territory for leverage and that I had no chance of getting through to him unless we were on neutral ground. So I had countered that we meet in a nearby conference room. We chatted for a few minutes about his background and I mentioned the case study I was working on, asking him a deliberately deferential question about his knowledge of the company in the case study. He held forth for a few minutes and it was clear that he knew what he was talking about. After that he asked rather briskly what this meeting was about. I explained that I had been asked to talk with him about how he was settling in at the company.

"Really? I have already been here six months and I would have thought that I *am* settled in, as you put it."

I replied that it might certainly seem so. "May I ask you, how do you think your working relationship with your peers here is going?"

"Why? Has someone been complaining?" Noble asked with a decided edge to his voice.

"Not exactly. But, let's set that aside for a moment and focus on my question to you. Your peer relationships?" He dryly explained that he could not truly be said to have any "peers per se" among the other executives due to the fact that he alone had extensive international business experience. That very acumen was the reason he had been brought on board. Nevertheless, he supposed that things were going about as well as could be expected. The clear implication was that he was doing the best he could among such backwoods provincials as our executive team.

I could have told him that one of our executives, Arnie, had recently been described in an industry magazine as a "rock star" in his area of expertise. He had endured a lot of good-natured ribbing from his colleagues over that one. But Arnie was one of the most humble and self-effacing men I had ever had the pleasure of working with, so he took it in stride. I could have added that another had recently met the president of the United States and that a third was former military intelligence. These men were nobody's fools. Instead, because this was not about them, but rather about Noble and whether he was going to be able to "make it" here, I asked him another uncomfortable question.

"Noble, does it concern you that you have not yet been able to form a single positive working relationship with any of your peers" (and I used the word deliberately) "in the six months you have been here?"

"Look," he said abruptly, "I'm not here to make friends. I'm here to make money, both for the company and for myself. I am not shy about that and I am pretty sure that is why they brought me in here."

"That could certainly be true." I acknowledged. "However, that only tells me why you think they brought you in. It does not tell me why you decided to join us, or whether you think it is working out well."

Slowly his self-assured façade, if indeed it was a façade, began to slip. His prior overseas job had ended in lay-offs, companywide he assured me, nothing personal and not reflective of his performance. His wife had been anxious to return to the states; and his son, who was at college, was having a little trouble, nothing serious of course, but a little concerning. The largest companies were mostly doing a little belt-tightening around the time of his lay-off, so he thought he would land for a bit in a smaller regional organization. Ours seemed to fill the bill. This move got him back in the states, allowed him to be close enough to check in from time to time on his son, and remain employed while planning his next career move.

This explained his indifference to whether he was forming decently effective work relationships. One, he felt so over-qualified for the job that it simply never occurred to him that he might not be succeeding at it; and two, the job itself held little interest for him, but rather it was a means to an end. He wanted to placate his wife, keep a closer eye on his troubled son, and he needed a job to pay the bills while he did those things. The job he currently held was a life-raft job, just something to tide him over a rough patch until he found something better – and most certainly bigger – to do.

In my bailiwick, this amounted to a near certain recipe for on-the-job failure. Carefully I told him that from the organization's perspective, things were not going as well as he seemed to think they were.

He asked for some examples and I provided them, demonstrating the need for him to become more cooperative within the executive group. He remained dismissive of any account that did not flatter his expertise. He was skeptical of my feedback and made it clear that he would check with a few others who "out-ranked" me to see whether I was off base.

"Could I ask you, who do you think you might check with?"

"Well, for starters, certainly Tom," (the CEO and Noble's direct superior) "and maybe a board member or two," Noble declared.

"I see. Then it will surprise you to learn that these are the very men who asked me to speak with you about this issue," I told him.

His initial reaction was complete disbelief, followed quickly by a slow-burn. I sensed fury rumbling just below the surface, and after a further brief exchange, wherein he made it clear that he was not interested in listening to anything else I might have to say, the meeting ended.

I walked slowly back to my own office, in an adjoining building on our corporate campus, asking myself, as I occasionally did in these frustrating moments, *what* did I think I was accomplishing? It was spring time, and the sidewalk between the two buildings was lined on both sides with trees in full bloom, showering the walkway with small white petals. However, their attractive appearance was largely negated by the fact that these trees, while blooming, gave off a strongly unpleasant odor. Most of us who worked there just called them "stinky trees" because none of us knew the name of that species. They were nice to look at, but you just didn't want to spend any time in close proximity to them. They reminded me of how most of his colleagues felt about Noble.

Then, as I walked I prayed, "*Lord, please help me to remember that this was not about me, but about Noble and what he is hoping to accomplish and about what the organization needs from him. Help me to do my best and leave the results up to you.*"

Easier said than done. Once again, I wish I could report that it got better for Noble, but it did not. The company let him go about three months later, with a modest severance package and no farewell luncheon. He was so universally disliked that no one would have attended.

On the week that he departed, a couple of other directors and a VP or two asked me casually in passing whether I had heard that "Noble got kicked to the curb this week?" I just nodded and kept moving. Only the CEO and the board of directors knew anything about my discussion with Noble a few months earlier, or about the debriefing I gave Tom, the CEO, the following day. Confidentiality in my line of work was critical, even after the fact. No one else within the organization would ever hear from me what the CEO had told me, the day he asked me to write up Noble's severance documents.

"It's a shame," Tom said to me. "He really does have some skills. But he doesn't have a clue."

The absence of self-awareness, in my observation, often became more acute the higher up the corporate ladder one climbed. It was worrisome, as I was now not far below the top level, and I did not want to fall into that same trap. What if I already had done so and simply did not know it? Then I remembered that I had a husband, three adult children, and two dogs, any one of whom would happily remind me that I had plenty of foibles of my own. In fact, they would gladly volunteer for such duty.

In twelve-step programs there is a principle that "awareness" is the key ingredient to staying sober and maintaining some life balance. Or so I have been told. Not a bad bit of advice for any of us. Hubris is such a destructive attitude and yet we can be so convinced of our own superiority that we drink our own Kool-Aid, congratulating ourselves that we thought to add the extra sugar.

Tending Tip:
- Confidential information can contain an energy all its own. To be in the know, to be aware of what is going to happen before it occurs, can be heady stuff. It is also heavy baggage. While it is understandable to take some pride in bearing the load for the good of the organization, keep in mind that at some point you will be told to lay it down. Or that inside knowledge will be given to someone else. Access to privileged information does not make one superior, only entrusted with a special burden.
- Integrity and honor will help you bear the burden of confidentiality. Humility will help you know when it is time to lay it down.

For whoever who exalts himself will be humbled, and whoever humbles himself will be exalted. – Matthew 23:12

Conclusion

Pulling Into The Station

There were now days when I looked around at my surroundings with nostalgia. It was still my job to keep the company trains running on time; but I could feel the tendency to cast a backward glance at the journey and reflect upon all that had transpired to bring me to this place. I would not be in charge much longer, as I was already mentoring my replacement, as this train was pulling into the station. Retirement was beckoning.

By this time I occupied a corner office. Of course, it was a two-story building so there were, in fact, eight corner offices. Still it made me smile when I remembered the week, a few years earlier, when I moved into these spacious quarters. I had resisted relocating from my perfectly adequate office just down the hall from the one I now occupied. I had stalled for two weeks after my promotion to vice president of HR; because I felt a little awkward moving into the rarified atmosphere of an executive space. Nonetheless, the CEO, to whom I now directly reported, had finally insisted that I get moving as "the optics mattered", or so he said.

The director of security and facility services, Chuck, had come to see me on the Friday evening before I was due to move into the new office the following Monday. "Hey, Marsha. How's it going? Congratulations by the way." Chuck was a friendly guy with an easygoing demeanor and by then we had worked together for years. "So what color would you like?"

"I'm sorry – what color would I like for what?" I asked him.

He laughed and replied, "What color would you like the walls in your new office painted? We can't replace the carpet, because that was just done last year. But you can have the walls done any color you like. Just tell me what you want and I'll get a crew in here over the weekend so that it will be ready for you Monday."

"That's really nice, but it isn't necessary. Whatever is on there will be fine."

"Nope. The other VPs all have personalized office décor and you should too." So he showed me a color chart with an acceptable range of "corporate colors" and come Monday my office had subdued blue walls and smelled like fresh paint. I had chosen a shade that was serene specifically because people coming into that particular office were sometimes nervous. This color had the added benefit of being gender neutral.

Although I did not think of myself as an intimidating person, experience had taught me that the job as the head of HR for the entire company (by this time around twelve hundred employees) carried with it a lot of positional power. I was careful to wear that mantle lightly and part of that meant making a concerted effort to put people at ease. I always sat with any visitors at a small conference table, never behind my desk like some kind of potentate; because as the reader may recall, I had experienced that treatment personally many years before this, and I had never forgotten how it made me feel.

Along a side wall I had a small fountain on the credenza, so the soothing sound of trickling water was always in the background. The wall art was beautiful and calming and I reminded myself every day when I walked into that space that I worked there, I did not rule there. I owned no scepter but I did have a very well-worn hoe. I had been tending people for a long time.

There had been a few occasions over the years when there had been some risks associated with the job. I remembered the time I was about to dismiss an employee (for serious cause) and I received an unexpected call from Chuck, earlier that morning. "Hey, Marsha, I hear you are going to have to fire that lunatic over in the call center later today. I'm going to assign someone to be right outside your office door during the termination meeting."

"Thanks, Chuck, but I don't think that will be necessary. I appreciate your concern though."

"Marsha, that guy is six foot two and weighs about two-seventy-five. And he has a reputation for having a bad temper. There will be somebody stationed in the hallway, just in case. Not up for discussion."

I glanced out the window where, just beyond the manicured shrubbery, my car sat in its reserved spot. Now there was a perk that was much to be desired and it again reminded me of Chuck's good services. The week after the painting episode, he had once again dropped by with a question. "Where do you want your parking spot to be?"

This time I at least knew what he was referring to, because every executive was assigned a reserved spot, with their last name painted on the curb in front of it. A few were located inside a fenced area with a gated key card entry. Others, however, were located in a spot near the exterior entrance closest to that executive's office. He suggested I take a spot inside the locked area. "I know you sometimes work late and leave when there is no one around. One of the nut-jobs you have had to let go might just decide to pay you a visit, so I think it would be safer to have you park inside the gated area."

I told him that I really appreciated his concern but the gated area was on the far side of the campus and was a long walk from my office. I had been parking out in the regular parking lot which was also a considerable distance from my office. However, there was a vacant spot very near this new office's outside entrance that would be much more convenient in bad weather or whenever I was carrying an armload of heavy files. Could I have that one?

Chuck hesitated, but saw the logic of what I was saying, so he compromised. "Okay, I guess that makes sense. But I don't like the idea that anyone can drive by and see your last name painted there and know that that is where you will come out to your car; especially now that you are an officer and your picture is on the company website as the head of HR. I am going to have them paint only your initials on it. It's not ideal but it is less noticeable and a little safer, I think."

I thanked him and the next day the "Reserved" sign went up and down on the curb were my initials. I no longer wore heels to work each day, reserving those torturous accessories for board meetings and the like. Still, how I appreciated that shortened trip to my car each evening at the end of a long day.

The perks of an executive position were beyond anything I had ever expected. My monthly car allowance was more than I had earned per month as salary in my job at the dental office. (Of course, that had been more than a quarter of a century ago. Talk about feeling the years creep up on you.) There were stock-options, stock-grants and bonuses. It all felt a little dizzying to me and not necessarily deserved. The day the Chief Financial Officer called me to his office to deliver my first stock grant, he had to explain the ramifications to me, like registering with the Securities and Exchange Commission (SEC) and filing something called an 8-K. I was just doing my job here like everyone else, so why should I be showered with such largesse? Although I was the lowest paid member on the executive team (HR often is) I still felt blessed beyond measure. And that said nothing of my expense account, which hardly bore thinking about. I tried to use that thing as little as possible, specifically because I had seen too many individuals over the years end up completely derailed with what had gone down into one of those slush ponds.

We executives were sometimes petted and feted until I was embarrassed to be part of it. I recalled walking into the top floor of a highrise office building on the harbor in Portland, Oregon. The view was stunning, meant to impress visitors. It did. It was an organization with which our pension fund had ongoing investment business and even by corporate standards the dining display on the conference room table was opulent. For once, I did not quite feel like the only rustic rube in the place; as the finance guy I had flown up with whistled and said, "That is the biggest platter of shredded crab meat I have ever seen in my life." It was enormous, standing about a foot high and at least two feet across. This mountain of meat was bracketed by at least two dozen accompanying dishes of salads, breads, fruit and cheese platters, and various desserts. I could only suppose they were planning to feed a visiting horde right after we few, we fattened few, had waddled out of the luncheon after dispatching a few tens of millions of dollars, along with about one quarter of the crab platter.

However, my reminiscences as I looked around that day were by no means limited to corporate indulgences. Mostly I remembered the men and women who had given me their trust and who had sometimes allowed me to mentor them. I thought fondly of the long tenured employee who had never received a promotion – not one – in over fifteen years. He was only slightly more elated than I was, when after some coaching, he received his first promotion. I recalled the young woman who wept as she acknowledged her wrong doing, but also acknowledged that she had learned from it and would not repeat her mistake in her next job.

Then there was the fellow who paid me what he considered a great compliment, when he declared that he was amazed that he was not bored during the mandatory ethics class I conducted. Granted it was not a high bar to clear, but I appreciated the thought. And yes, I recalled the few who had threatened me with mayhem on their way out the door. Where were they now, I wondered? But I savored the memories of the "thank you-s" and found they meant so much more to me than the few who had said something like, "Who do you think you are?"

Not everyone is called to tend people. It is a hard calling, to be sure. It can be exhausting and heartbreaking. But the opportunity to be of some real use in the world, especially in an arena where others are striving to earn their living, pay their mortgages, and feed their families; that is a rare gift. Who wouldn't love an opportunity like that?

And so, very soon now, would come the farewell tour: last staff meetings, good bye luncheons, and the big retirement bash. There would be a big cake, a few small gifts, and my assistant, Jill, had been working in semi-secret on a memory album of my career with the company.

I had been meeting with and mentoring my soon-to-be successor, Dora, who was an executive director in another area of the company. She was talented at things I knew little about, like investor relations and earnings calls. She had no real experience in human resources, but the powers that be had selected her over the guy I had recommended for the position. He was my second-in-command, steadfast and unassuming, but he knew HR inside out and upside down. The CEO had acknowledged to me that he had a political agenda when he chose Dora, so I was overruled. (Some things never changed.) Still, I wanted to give Dora the best chance for success that I could. During one of the last times we met she seemed hesitant and unsure of herself. This was unusual because she was bright, hard-working, and ambitious. After we had covered the routine matters of the week, I asked her if everything was all right.

"I just don't know if I can do this job." Dora said.

I immediately wondered what I had left undone or unexplained, so I asked her, "Is there some area of the job that I have over looked sharing with you? I mean, I realize employment law is a real labyrinth, but you can always call legal for advice. And as for compensation and benefits, you've got that down cold. Training you can often delegate. So are there things you want to ask me about that we haven't gotten to yet?"

"No, it's not that. It is just that ..." she hesitated a moment, "it's just that you are beloved all over the company. And I just don't know how to follow that."

I assured her that she was going to do just fine and ended the meeting as quickly as I could. I was deeply moved and I did not want her to see how touched I was. As soon as I was alone tears filled my eyes. I could not help it – beloved? I was beloved? I never knew, never suspected. But I was humbled and grateful. What an experience this journey had been. For me, my career had also been a calling. And it had been a privilege–this business of tending people.

I am going to presume upon the reader's forbearance just a moment or two longer and add a few final thoughts for your consideration. There is a common misperception that the need for confidentiality in dealing with others is really about secrecy. It is not. Neither is it about being one-up on someone or having covert leverage over others. Those who perceive confidentiality in such terms should be viewed with great caution. If you interview with an organization and suspect there are "secret games" being played (and such organizations will often tip their hand even as early as the interview process) run, do not walk, to the nearest exit.

If you have a dawning awareness that you already work in an organization that uses the requirement for confidentiality as a means for exerting undue pressure or self-serving influence, for maintaining the privilege of the few at the expense of the many, then you have a choice to make. You can decide to try to change things for the better from the inside out, or you can decide that you need to walk away for the sake of your own integrity. I have done both during my career and in neither case was the path an easy one. Only you can decide which road is right for you in that specific situation. What I would encourage you to do is to face the issue head on and *make* a decision. To punt, to go along to get along, is to begin to poison your own character. It will not be worth it in the end.

Confidentiality, when used rightly, is really about just one or two things: respect for others and the impact confidential information may have upon them, and the appropriate timing of the disclosure of such knowledge. Respect and timing, that's it. Anything else is more than likely a cloak for something other than what it purports to be. Because confidentiality plays such a large role in in tending people, it is important to keep this in mind.

Given you have read this far, I assume that you either earn your living tending people or you are interested in doing so at some point. Good for you, because there is a tremendous need for those who are willing to tend to others. Frankly, many people in companies, clubs, churches and civic organizations have been "managed and motivated" nearly to exhaustion. They are hungry for someone who might show a genuine interest in them as a person, rather than as just one more cog in the works.

As you have already learned in these chapters, it is not an easy way to make a living. But it can be a rewarding one if you are willing to go the extra mile (or two), if you see value in helping others achieve their own goals and dreams, and if you find satisfaction in knowing you made a real difference in someone's life.

I have great respect for everyone who simply does the best they know to do on a daily basis, regardless of what the job entails. To "suit up and show up" is always half the battle. As you make that daily choice, remember to take care of yourself and to tend to others with kindness as you have opportunity.

Final Tending Tip: Do the right thing, the right way (again–as often as you can figure out what that is) and the right things will usually come your way. Maybe not right away, but sooner or later they may very well come your way.

But seek first the kingdom of God and his righteousness and all these things will be added to you. –Matthew 6:33

Notes

1. Nouwen, Henri J.M. *Reaching Out: The Three Movements of the Spiritual Life*. (New York, N.Y.: Doubleday, 1995), Kindle edition, Location 92.
2. *Webster's New World Dictionary: Third College Edition*. Ed. Victoria Neufeldt and David B. Guralnik. (New York, N.Y.: Prentice Hall, 1994), 1378.
3. DePree, Max, *Leadership Is An Art*. (New York, N.Y.: Dell Publishing, 1989), 60.
4. Franklin, Benjamin. https://www.fi.edu>benjamin-franklin>-famous-quotes. Accessed April, 2021.
5. https://en.wikipedia.org/wiki/Keep_Calm_and_Carry_On. Accessed July 7, 2021.
6. Addictioncenter.com/addiction/workplace. Author Jeffrey Juergens, July 3, 2019. Accessed April 3, 2021.
7. Greenleaf, Robert K., *On Becoming a Servant Leader*. ed. Don M. Frick and Larry C. Spears, (San Francisco, CA: Jossey-Bass, 1996), 97.
8. Likert, Rensis. https://questionpro.com/blog/rensis_likert_and_the_likert_scale/. Accessed on March 4, 2021.
9. Peck, M.Scott, *A World Waiting to Be Born: Civility Rediscovered*. (New York, N.Y.: Bantam Books, 1993), 251.

10. DeRusha, Michelle, *50 Women Every Christian Should Know: Learning From Heroines of the Faith.* (Grand Rapids, MI: Baker Books, 2014), 37.
11. Elton Trueblood, *A Place to Stand: A Practical Guide to Christianity in Changing Times.* (New York, N.Y.: Harper Collins Publisher, 1969), Kindle Edition, location 1213.
12. Brians, Prof. Paul, website article: *discretion is the better part of valor.* https://brians.wsu.edu.>2016/05/25>discretion-is-the-better-part-of-valor. Shakespeare's Henry IV, Part 1, Scene 3, lines 3085-3086. Accessed July 19, 2021.
13. Greenleaf, *On Becoming a Servant Leader*, 151.
14. Roosevelt, Theodore Quotes, https://brainyquote.com/authors/theodore-roosevelt-quotes. Accessed March 15, 2021.

Bibliography

Brians, Prof. Paul. Website article. https://brians.wsu.edu. discretion-is-the-better-part-of-valor. May 2016

DePree, Max. *Leadership Is An Art*. New York, NY: Dell Publishing, 1989

DeRusha, Michelle. *50 Women Every Christian Should Know: Learning From Heroines of the Faith*. Grand Rapids, MI: Baker Books, 2014

Franklin, Benjamin. https://www.fi.edu>benjamin-franklin->famous-quotes. April 2021

Greenleaf, Robert K. *On Becoming a Servant Leader*. Edited by Don M. Frick and Larry C. Spears. San Francisco, CA: Jossey-Bass, 1996

Juergens, Jeffrey. https://www.com/Addictioncenter.com/addiction/workplace. April 2021

Keep Calm and Carry On. https://en.wikipedia.org/wiki/Keep_Calm_and_Carry_On. July 2021.

Likert, Rensis. *Rensis Likert and the Likert Scale.* https://www.questionpro.com/blog/rensis_likert_and_the_likert_scale/. March 2021

Neufeldt, Victoria and Guralnik, David B. *Webster's New World Dictionary: Third College Edition.* New York, N.Y.: Prentice Hall, 1994.

Nouwen, Henri J.M. *Reaching Out: The Three Movements of the Spiritual Life.* New York, N.Y.: Doubleday, 1995

Peck, M. Scott. *A World Waiting to Be Borne: Civility Rediscovered.* New York, NY: Bantam Books, 1993

Roosevelt, Theodore Quotes. https://brainyquote.com/authors/theodore-roosevelt-quotes. March 2021

Trueblood, D. Elton. *A Place to Stand: A Practical Guide to Christianity in Changing Times,* New York, N.Y.: Harper Collins, 1969

About the Author

Marsha Young worked for many years in human resources management in both small and large organizations. Her career spanned assignments beginning in employee relations and recruitment, included several years working in a Fortune 500 company, and culminated in serving as the Vice-President of Human Resources in a mid-sized corporation listed on the NASDAQ.

She holds a master's degree in human resources and was certified as an SPHR (Senior Professional in Human Resources), as well as being a certified corporate trainer and ethics instructor. She is a seasoned speaker at business and civic functions, sharing her experiences and insights with humor and discretion.

She currently lives in Northern California with her husband and their dog, Dusty.